FREE GIFT
by
PAWAWARE

FOLLOW THE LINK BELOW TO GET A FREE GIFT BY US THAT WILL SURELY HELP YOU IN YOUR JOURNEY TO TRAIN YOUR DOG!

SCAN
ME

www.pawaware.com/Gift

Foreword

This book is written for young adults to encourage them to participate in a positive, healthy and environment friendly activity. This is a common observation that having a pet makes a family and a person less stressful. In the wake of COVID-19 pandemic, its importance has significantly increased as we are confined to our limited social circle. The main objective is to introduce the kids to the wonderful world of having and taking care of a pet. It also inculcates some really useful habits like punctuality, empathy, observation, physical exercise and patience. If you enjoy having fun time with your pet, I would think that my purpose of writing this book is served. Don't forget to be responsible and have a lot of fun!

How to use this book

The whole book is divided into sections, so you could go straight to the section you are interested in. The section most commonly you would use might be 'House Training', 'Obedience Training', 'Cool Tricks' and 'Fun and Games'. All the activities mentioned in these chapters have three parts; first, the things you need to perform a particular activity, second, the steps that you must take to perform the activity and finally, some troubleshooting tips on hazards or what to do when things go wrong along with some safety tips. First, focus on the 'House Training' and then move forward. Don't try to teach too many tricks at a time, add more tricks when your puppy becomes master of the basics. In the 'You Need' section, you might notice some previous activities that are required.

A note on Pronouns

Most people don't like to refer to their pet as 'it', they tend to treat their pet more like a family member. So, I have decided to use the plural pronoun, 'they', 'them', 'their' or 'she' , 'her' as the pronoun of choice.

Table of Contents

Introduction

Human-dog relationship

The relation between humans and dogs is so old that we can't even trace it back in time. We might not know the exact date but we know for sure that a dog has been a faithful companion of humans and its ancestors. Humans kept dogs to hunt, guard, and to entertain themselves. The people who pet a dog generally become more empathetic, caring and close to the nature. Investing in this relationship is always a good idea. Since you have decided to pet a dog early in your life this would be a great experience for your personality grooming. Humans have learnt a lot from the dogs like loyalty, passion, being active, being consistent and many cool habits to name a few. This book will help you strengthen your relationship by guiding you on how to train your puppy, to make it part of your life and by giving you an idea that how much time and effort might be required.

Children and puppies

Puppies are kids; so they are energetic, loving, innocent and curious just like human kids. They get along pretty well with humans as long as you understand their needs and help them with it. As a responsible caregiver you would not only play with her but also take good care of her needs. You have to visualize that you have adopted her from her family, so now you are her family.

Puppy Socializing and Exploring

The first 4 months in your puppy's social life are very important. As she will learn a lot about the world and the people around her. She would become familiar with the surroundings, people and objects. This is your opportunity to 'make friends' with her and 'show her around'. Make her comfortable with your house and everything in it. Take her out and let her experience the nature. These initial months will bring her up to be a confident adult. In short you want to her to play a lot

cause her stress or fear. In natural environment any animal's parents act as their guardians and safe keep them from dangers and other animals until they are on their own. Here you are; the caregiver and guardian of your puppy. Prepare a lot of fun things for your puppy while keeping it safe. For instance, during exploration you puppy might jump into a garbage can and doesn't find a way to come out due to slippery surface. She might get close to a hot stove. She walks carelessly on the road while chasing a butterfly. You have to be close by to look after her.

Let your puppy meet all sorts of cool people. She needs to get familiar with all kinds of varieties of people. She can guess their intentions instinctively but the visuals you have to provide. Introduce her to people one by one. Imagine yourself surrounded by 'giants' gathered around you trying to pat you or talk to you. She could get scared as well. Once she is familiar with humankind, then you can let her meet as many people as you wish. Why is it important to introduce your puppy to variety of people? Most dogs when they meet a human who is different from others in their attire, they fail to put them in the 'humans' category and would either bark or run away from them. You should set a target of 1-2 new people every day. You also want your puppy to have a good first meeting experience with them. You have to explain your friends and neighbors not to overwhelm your puppy by patting and hugging. Keep some treats handy and ask them to offer treat to your puppy. Just let her hang around them and when she feels comfortable enough, only then she'd get closer. If she shows signs of discomfort, take her away. Don't let them treat her like an object and pick it up, hug her or kiss her. Keep your puppy away from pranksters who like to scare your puppy with scary sounds or aggressive actions. This will reduce her confidence in you and in humans in general.

Puppies like to play with others of their kind. Make sure some adult supervises their interaction with other puppies all the time. Don't let her mingle with stray dogs as vaccination is important. Some adult dogs don't like to play with puppies so if the dogs show signs of dislike (showing teeth, turning away and stiffening) take her somewhere else.

Everyone has a personal space bubble. You like to keep your distance especially with strangers. Dogs have that bubble too. They can be scared of the objects too. Let's say your puppy doesn't like the shape of a mural in your house and shows sign of discomfort, take her away from it. If she is scared of the sound of a vacuum cleaner, take her to other room and give her time to figure out by herself that it is not dangerous.

Dogs are not visual animals but their nose makes up for it. That's why they recognize people from their smell more than their visuals. So, if you are wearing a mask, a helmet, large sunshades or have a new hairdo, she might fail to recognize you from a distance. Even when you get close, she might still be confused that it smells like my friend but doesn't look like it. So, part of the training is to make sure she recognizes you in every form; whether you are wearing heavy winter clothes or carrying a schoolbag.

This exploration phase should include different objects such as cars, bicycles, television, cellphones, books, washing machines, dishwashers, microwave ovens, sofas, tables and even the paintings and decoration pieces.

Why a puppy needs to be trained?

Training is an important part of every dog's life for several reasons. Without proper training, your puppy wouldn't be a lot of fun to be around. You won't be able to properly communicate with her and thus fail in sustaining a long-term friendship. So, if you want to have lots of fun with your puppy and maintain a nice and friendly relationship with her, proper training is the key. Experts say that training a puppy (a year or two old) is relatively much easier than an adult dog. This is because puppies are in their learning phase, and thus take in everything you teach them much easily and quickly. Moreover, they don't have any permanent negative behaviors and habits while an untrained adult dog is likely to. While it's still possible to train an adult dog to abandon negative traits and be obedient, it requires more time and hard work. So, the best practice is to start training your puppy as soon as possible.

How taking care of your puppy is the owner's responsibility

When you purchase or adopt a puppy or any other pet, you agree to take full responsibility for all her needs and treat her nicely. You should only own a pet if you are capable enough to give her proper time, facilities, and attention. Otherwise, you may hand these responsibilities to someone else e.g. a dog sitter or a doggy daycare.

Now, when you are accepting the responsibility of a puppy, you have to provide her with their basic needs like food, water, and shelter along with other requirements such as toys, medical services, vaccination, grooming, training, walking, and above all your dedicated attention.

How much attention and efforts are required in this?

Initially, it might be daunting for you to consider having a pet. It requires a lot of work, time, dedication, and commitment. If you feel that it is too much for you to keep up with this responsibility along with your studies and other activities, it is a good idea to share the responsibilities with your family. If you have any siblings, you may share the puppy with them, this way, you can all enjoy along with dividing the responsibilities amongst yourselves. A good way to do this is using a daily or weekly chart as the examples shown below:

Weekly	
Monday	Mum, Jo
Tuesday	Ann, Dad
Wednesday	Jo, Ann
Thursday	Dad, Jo
Friday	Mum, Ann
Saturday	Mum, Dad
Sunday	Ann, Jo

Daily	
Responsibility	**Person**
Morning Walk	Dad
Breakfast	Ann
Training	Jo, Mum
Afternoon walk	Ann
Dinner	Jo
Sleep, Cleaning up	Dad, Mum

You can make up a timetable that suits you depending on each of your family member's routine and other daily activities. It would be a good idea to shuffle activities amongst yourselves so that everyone can enjoy different things and no one gets bored of doing repetitive tasks.

BOXER

POODLE

SHEPHERD

RETRIEVER

MITTELSCHNAUZER

LABRADOR

PITBULL

DOG BREEDS

DALMATIAN

DOBERMAN

GREAT DANE

WHIPPET

RIESENSCHNAUZER

SETTER

DACHSHUND

BASSET NAUND

Getting a new dog

Find a suitable breed

The following section compares seven dog breed groups to help you decide between them if you are planning to get a new puppy. Remember, you can skip this section if you have already got a puppy.

Herding dogs

Herding dogs were originally bred to help shepherds in herding animals. They are very intelligent, loyal, and are great family pets. However, as they are very active, they are likely to cause mischief if aren't provided enough daily exercise.

Guard dogs

Guard dogs are known for their loyalty, and physical strength. They are calm and gentle, but their guarding senses make them rather unpredictable. Some breeds belonging to the guarding group tend to be less family friendly, so it is recommended to think twice before getting a guard dog for children.

Work Dogs

Work dogs are physically strong and need a lot of physical exercise and mental stimulation. They might not be considered as the perfect family pets because of their demand of excessive physical work.

Terriers

Terries are active and playful. They can be fun to watch and play with. Originally, they were bred as farm dogs for repelling foxes and other animals.

Toy Dogs

Toy dogs are known to be cute, lovely, and affectionate. They are very friendly and playful which makes them fun to be around. Some of the toy dogs, like poodles have special grooming requirements. Toy dogs have a chance of becoming too much connected to one person and can later be uncomfortable, or worse, aggressive towards other people. So, they need to be properly socialised with plenty of people and other dogs and animals.

Hounds

Hounds were originally bred for hunting. They have strong hunting instincts. Sight hounds have a sharp eye sight and can take off after anything in motion, which can make them tough to walk with. Scent hounds have a strong sense of smell and can track prey by its scent. Similar to sight hounds they may wander off towards anything that smells 'interesting'. This makes them rather difficult to train.

Sporting Dogs

Sporting dogs generally are family-friendly. They are very active, so need proper regular exercise. They love people and are great pets. They enjoy long walks and runs, along with other field activities.

Welsh Corgi	Siberian Husky	Dachshund	Beagle
Rottweiler	Pug	Akita Inu	Jack Russell Terrier
Pomeranian	Dalmatian	Chihuahua	Golden Retriever
Doberman Pinscher	Saint Bernard	Shih Tzu	Riesenschnauzer

Some of the popular family-friendly breeds

Breed name	Weight (in lbs.)	Height (in inches)	Grooming Requirements	Activity Requirement	Barking	Description
Golden Retriever	55-75	21-24	Needs weekly brushing, no special needs	Needs lots of activity	Not unnecessarily	Golden retrievers are devoted, friendly, playful, and intelligent, thus easier to train
Labrador Retriever	55-80	21.5-24.5	Weekly Brushing	Needs lots of activity	Medium	Labrador retrievers are a popular breed. They belong to the sporting group.
Poodle	50-70	15	Needs a lot of grooming/ professional services	Not much	Medium	Poodles are smart, fancy, and active.
Irish Setter	60-70	25-27	Brushing every 2-3 days	Lots of activity	Medium	Irish setters are sweet-natured, very active dogs.
Vizsla	44-60	21-24	Weekly Brushing	Energetic	Medium	Vizsla is a gentle, affectionate and loving breed.
Newfoundland	100-150	26-28	Weekly Brushing	Regular exercise	When necessary	Newfoundland are sweet, devoted, and patient.
Border Collie	30-55	18-22	Brushing 2-3 times a week	Needs lots of activity	Medium	Border collies are family-friendly gentle, smart and active dogs.
Bull terrier	50-70	20-22	Weekly brushing	Energetic	Medium	Bull terriers are playful and may need a yard. They can have mischief in their mind sometimes.
Bull dog	40-50	14-15	Brushing twice a week	Regular exercise	Infrequent	Bull dogs are friendly and courageous.
Beagle	20-30	13-15	Brushing 2-3 times a week	Energetic	Frequently	Beagles are also pretty friendly but are also fairly curious.
Pug	14-18	10-13	Weekly brushing	Regular exercise	When necessary	Pugs are loving and cute, but can be mischievous sometimes.
Papillion	5-10	8-11	Weekly brushing	Regular exercise	Barks a lot	Papillion is a cute, and friendly breed but they do bark a lot.

Points to consider when choosing the right puppy

 You should consult other family members before choosing a dog. Compare different breed groups with information such as weight range, size, behavior and special abilities. Perform a self-analysis and decide based on your personal preference based on your home environment, lifestyle, daily routine, and family members. There are several things you might want to consider when choosing a dog. First thing that matters the most is the size of your house and yard. Next thing that you should consider is that how much time would your puppy be home alone.

There are no fixed rules but you can use the following questions as starting point. These questions can help you decide.

- 🐾 What breed are you interested in?
- 🐾 What should be the age of your dog/puppy? (a puppy is usually between six months and two years, below is a new-born and above is an adult dog)
- 🐾 What is the energy level of your chosen dog? (more energy means more space to exercise e.g., terriers are more active and alert than toy dogs
- 🐾 What is the grooming requirement? (poodles and other 'fancy' breeds require regular haircuts and trims which is an extra responsibility/expense, and avoid ones with hair or fur if you are allergic to these.)
- 🐾 What kind of house do you have? Do you have a lot of decoration? Or is there a lot of glass?
- 🐾 You should think about how safe your neighborhood is.
- 🐾 How much can you spend on your puppy per week?
- 🐾 How many grooming trips can you manage?
- 🐾 How much walk/exercise can you give your puppy daily?
- 🐾 How much time can you invest in training your puppy?
- 🐾 Do you have other pets (especially cats) at your house?

Preparing for the dog's arrival

Prepare your house to be suitable for a dog

You have decided which puppy you are getting and from where, now is the time to make some preparations for your new friend to arrive. Some background work is required for the big day to make your new friend feel welcomed. Remember you are about to enter a long-term relationship with your friend so we will do our best to make her feel comfortable. Find and assign a place for the crate that is in your reach and you can quickly spot if your friend is missing.

Set a potty spot for your puppy beforehand, so you will not have to do it in a hurry.

When your puppy would arrive, they would be in exploration mode so keep your valuables out of reach and out of sight of your puppy. She would not be able to differentiate between a valuable vase and a 'shining toy'. There are a number of items that can harm her such as chemical products perceived as edible, toys that make sudden noise, small objects causing a choking hazard.

Basically, you would 're-visit' your house from her point of view. If possible, survey the house on all-four to visualize what would be visible for her. Check if they have free access to the kitchen, try to restrict it. If you don't have a kitchen door, get some obstacles, as unnoticed entry of your puppy into the kitchen can cause serious accidents. Some common food items are dangerous for your puppy such as grapes, nuts, raisins, avocado and chocolate.

Look out for hanging/wall mounted objects like paintings, stereo system, television. Can your puppy knock them off? If so, then secure them well, place them higher (out of sight) or remove them for some time until she is familiar.

If you have other pets consider their options of co-living with a puppy and can you separate their living spaces?

You need to find a veterinarian /veterinary doctor and a grooming salon nearby. Consider ones that are close to your house, so you can go to them immediately in case of emergencies. You need to get her vaccinated (if not already vaccinated) and should consult a vet for necessary guidelines and assistance for your puppy's health. You should ask around other pet owners about recommendations.

You might be too excited to let your friends meet your puppy but don't call them on the very first day of her arrival! She might be scared to see so many of your friends trying to pet her. Call your friends when she has settled in.

If you put yourself in her shoes, you'll know that visiting a hospital might not be a cozy experience. You can make such visits as stress-free as possible by following these steps.

Visit the veterinarian waiting room even if you don't have an appointment. This will make your pup feel home and reduce anxiety on the next visits. This is not a social visit so make sure strangers don't touch her and don't let her interact with other pets as it can increase her fear and anxiety.

Ask the previous owner and get her vaccinated for common diseases. Do take her for regular checkups.

If the veterinary doctor asks you to hold your puppy, don't hold it too tight. Your objective is to comfort her as much as you can.

Dog accessories

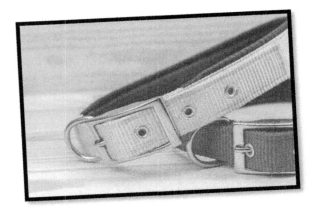

Collar and tag

Collar, with a name tag and other information such as your phone number and house address, and a leash hook.

A dog collar is an essential accessory for your puppy as it would have your dog's name tag, and your phone number and house address that would be crucial if the puppy gets lost. Then, you would also need something to hook the leash onto, so, a collar is a must.

There are different types of collars available at pet stores. We recommend adjustable collars as some puppies' heads are smaller than their necks, so a standard collar would slip out. Then an adjustable collar would also be usable when the dog grows up (unless of course it snaps). If you can spend a couple extra dollars, you can have your and/or your dog's name, and your phone number engraved on the collar. Otherwise, you can simply attach a tag to it. The most common materials for collars are nylon and leather, both being fairly strong.

An alternative for the neck collar is the back-clip harness, that fits the dog's chest and clips on to the back. However, it is not recommended for puppies because it encourages pulling which will be a problem in loose-leash walk training (where you'd be training your puppy NOT to pull).

A dog training clicker

A small device that makes a clicking sound every time a button is pressed. They are available at most pet accessories shops at low prices and are otherwise easily available to buy online on Amazon for under $4.99. They are used in 'clicker training' (which will be covered later in this book) and basically, they just tune your puppy to hear a clicking sound every time they do as you wished. This will make it easy for them to know if their cations were right or wrong.

Clickers come in a lot of different shapes, sizes, and colors. You should choose a clicker that is comfortable in your hand and you can press it several times during training without strain. Some clickers have wrist straps while others have finger loops. It would be good to have something like this so that you can hold other stuff like treats in the same hand.

Another thing to keep in mind is the loudness of the clicker. If your dog has a hearing problem, or you hold your training sessions in a noisy area, you should go for the loud and harsh clickers. However, if your puppy is noise sensitive and startles at sudden noises, then you should keep a gentle and soft clicker.

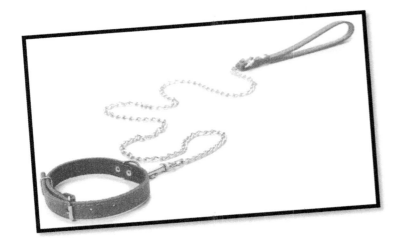

Leash

For puppies, a leash about 4-6 feet long would be fine. It is not recommended to use a retractable leash with puppies because it teaches them to pull which is a bad habit, so avoid retractable leashes. Leather and nylon leashes are stronger and less likely to snap than other fabrics. Although puppies usually can't pull hard enough to snap a leash, adjustable.

leashes are a better choice. If your puppy has started to chew through toys and leashes, you should look for a thick, wide, tightly-webbed nylon leash to protect it from being torn by chewing.

Walking tools
Other walking tools include harnesses, which come in different shapes and sizes. They are best for dogs already leash-walking trained, otherwise it would give your dog or puppy more pulling power which will make it difficult for you to walk them.

Food containers
Look for bowls that are easily movable. They must have a strong base to prevent tipping and

spilling. Prefer shapes that are handy to rinse and wash frequently. Plastic bowls are less costly than other options and are fairly durable, but can be easily chewed (if you puppy has started to) and scratched. This is unsafe as it would result in places for germs to build up. Moreover, a minority of dogs tend to have an allergy to plastic, and can have a skin reaction when in contact with it. So, try to lower your preference for plastic bowls.

Ceramic bowls are stylish and easy to clean, most being dish-washer safe. However, they can easily shatter if dropped, and can crack or chip on impact making them unsafe for your puppy. If you choose ceramic bowls, make sure to handle them carefully and check regularly for damage.

Stainless steel bowls are cheap, durable and easy to clean. Almost all of them are dish-washer safe and some have no-skid bottoms to prevent tipping and spilling. They do have their drawbacks though, they can develop stain and rust, especially if used outdoors. Avoid them if your puppy chews through stuff as chewing a steel bowl would damage their teeth. You may find steel bowls to be dull, boring, as they don't come in a variety of colors or designs.

Elevated dog bowls are typically two standard bowls attached to a stand about 12 inches high. They are suitable for giant adult dogs and are not suitable for puppies due to their height.

Automatic bowls have a normal bowls attached to a large container. The less costly ones just keep the bowls full at all times. They are not very appropriate for food as your puppy might overeat her food. For water however, it is a good choice as your puppy will have a constant supply of water at all times. There are more expensive options that allow you to program the feeding time and amount and it will automatically fill the bowl as per the defined limit. This is a good option if you are unable to feed your dog in person because for example, if you go to school in the morning. Remember to choose ones that are tamper proof.

If you like to take your puppy along often, you should keep a travel bowl too. These are made of light-weight fabrics and can be folded to smaller sizes once empty. They are extremely portable and are much handier than taking a standard bowl along on for example a trip to the park.

Another type of portable bowl are silicon bowls. These are great if you don't need them to store food, just for feeding. They are somewhat height adjustable and can be collapsed to a flat design after use. Some have clips or hooks so they can be attached to a bag or belt. The only problem is durability. They can be easily destroyed by a dog and should not be left around when not in use.

If your puppy shows excessive haste in eating, or just gulps down food without proper chewing, slow-feed bowls are the solution for that. They are specially designed to prevent a dog from taking in huge chunks and eating fast. They have sort of obstacles in the bowl in which the food is placed. They will help your puppy eat their food slowly and better enjoy meals.

First aid and emergency kit

You should always keep a first aid and emergency kit for your puppy. You should take it along when going outdoors for a significant amount of time e.g., a road trip. There are ready-made medical kits available specifically for dogs but you can make your own. Some of the most common objects you should have in your puppy medical kit and their respective uses are:

- Bandages: Bandages are used to cover open wounds and cuts so that harmful germs don't find their way into the body.

- Medical tape: Medical tape may be used to hold the bandage or other dressing on the wound in case of an injury.

- Gauze: Gauze is used to stop bleeding and keep open wounds, burns, or cuts clean.

- Antibiotic spray: Antibiotic spray is a standard dis-infectant spray that kills most harmful bacteria.

- Extra food and treats: These are important if you run out of your puppy's normal food supply or if you need to control your puppy using treats.

- Syringe: Syringe is used for flushing small sized wounds and/or feeding medications.

- Hydrogen per oxide: This chemical is a strong disinfectant and kills a lot of bacteria and viruses instantly.

- Milk of magnesia: It is used in case of a sour stomach and provides gastric relief.

- Activated charcoal: It is commonly used to treat poisonings.

It is a good practice to keep an extra leash and collar with you when you take your puppy on a trip. The emergency kit must include all your puppy's documents, medical records, and a dog first aid booklet. You should learn to use these different items beforehand so that you can handle them properly in case of an emergency.

Enclosed pet carriers

Enclosed pet carriers come in various sizes and designs. You should choose one that is suitable for your puppy. Prefer those with proper ventilations

Crate or other confinement space

The confinement space is a designated area in your house like backyard or laundry area that can be used to keep your puppy safe. It can be a crate where the puppy can spend 'me time'. The puppy should feel comfortable and at home in her crate. Nobody should disturb her not even for play in her space so that she would feel secure. The size and type of crate depends on the size of your puppy. The size of crate must be able to accommodate your puppy keeping in mind that she will grow soon.

Car safety restraints like a dog seat belt

Your puppy's safety is very important during car travel. You should get a var seat belt for her which will keep her secure not only in case of an accident but also during sharp turns and braking. The seat belt will also keep the driver distraction free as the dog won't be able to move here and there.

You should always accompany your young puppy in the car. Make sure not to leave her unattended. Keep her in an enclosed pet carrier and don't let her be unsecured. Her safety is important just like ours.

Dog ID tag

You should always give your puppy an ID tag with their name and your contact information such as phone number and house address. It is essential for her safety. You can also get a microchip ID for your puppy. The chip, containing vital information is embedded under the skin by a vet and is read by a special scanner. In case your puppy gets lost and is found by and animal shelter, the staff will scan the microchip if the ID tag is missing. Ask your parents' opinion about it.

Grooming and hygiene equipment

Grooming is essential to keep your puppy clean and healthy. It involves brushing, bathing, trimming nails, ear cleaning and brushing teeth. Depending on your puppy's breed, her grooming requirements will vary. Fancy breeds like poodles require weekly visits to the groomer.

If you choose to do all or part of the grooming by yourself with the help of an adult, you will need some equipment. It is important to leave the more difficult parts such as ear and mouth cleaning to an adult. There are many types of equipment available in different price ranges, you can choose those suitable for your puppy's demand. Some items you might need are hair brush, tooth brush, nail clipper, shampoo, conditioner, etc.

Grooming and hygiene equipment like brush, nail clipper, shampoo, conditioner, toothbrush, etc.

Toys

As puppies have an active and playful nature as they are developing, they need some interesting stuff to keep them stimulated and engaged. There are various types of toys available for puppies that can provide healthy entertainment for them.

Chew toys are very useful to train your puppy not to chew on things such as shoes and clothes. You will be providing a toy to fulfil their chewing desires with so they don't damage their teeth chewing harmful objects.

Chew toys come in different shapes and sizes. You should choose one that is suitable for your puppy depending on her size and personality. You should also consider the hardness of the toy. If your puppy has small weak teeth, a soft toy would be better. Otherwise, if she has big powerful teeth, a soft toy might get shredded and swallowed, so a harder one would be more suitable.

Treat Pouch

A treat pouch is a small bag that is used to hold treats and/or dog food. They come in various sizes; you can select one of your choice. A nice option would be one with a wrist band so you can free a hand from holding the pouch during training.

The first days

Introduce your home using a leash and remember to skip the places you don't want the dog to be sneaking in when you aren't around, for example the kitchen.

Let them meet with other pets especially other dogs and cats while on the leash. They would take some time to get comfortable with each other.

Let your puppy get comfortable at your home and wait a couple of days to take them out to show around the neighborhood.

You must be eager to introduce your pet to your friends and relatives, but remember, you need to give the puppy a rest. They have gone through a huge change, so give them time to settle down and wait until you aren't a total stranger to them. After a week or so, you can show them to your friends and family.

Divide puppy care responsibilities between family members and siblings using a walk chart. For example, Dad may do the morning walk, Mum can manage the breakfast. You and Mum can do the training, then some of your siblings (if any) can do the afternoon walk and the other can clean their crate.

Food and Treats

Choose a suitable and healthy dog food for your puppy and ask your friends and family who own a dog. There are many types of different dog foods available. Some of them are given below:

1. Kibble/Dry food
2. Canned
3. Home Cooked
4. Raw

Kibble and dry food are the most budget friendly option for your dog. It can be kept for a long time before it is expired and does not need to be refrigerated.

Homemade dried beef tail

Raw vs. Dry food

Canned Food

Using treats appropriately for training

1. Train your dog to take treats gently.

2. Give her treats from your hand rather than dropping it on the floor to keep her from losing focus and be attentive to you.

3. Keep a sufficient number of treats in a pouch beforehand so you can easily and quickly reward her.

4. For the puppy, use smaller sized treats, so, giving a lot of treats wouldn't upset her stomach.

5. Let the treats be a reward. Don't give them treats as food. Let your puppy know that she will only get a treat when she does something right.

Use high-value and low-value treats as mentioned with the activity. Basically, high-value treats are those which are loved by your puppy and she'll be willing to do anything in order to earn it. They are used in the more advanced exercises. Examples of high-value treats are:

Healthy raw food ingredients

- Cooked meat
- Chicken
- Sausage
- Beef
- Liver
- Tuna
- Cheese

Low-value treats are those which your puppy is eager to eat and will do simple stuff to get it, but will not be as excited about it compared to high-value treats. Examples of low-value treats are:

- Dog Biscuit
- Small chunks of some fruit or vegetable e.g. apple, carrot.
- Dry dog food/Kibble

Using a clicker along with treats

During training sessions, remember to click and treat every time your puppy does what you wanted her to. This will tune her that there is a click every time she does something you like and get a reward (treat). It is important that you click at the right moment to make it easy for your puppy to learn the pattern of click and treat. You can ask your friend or family member to clap their hands and try to match the click with it. Later you can try with something faster, like bouncing a ball. Better to change the clap and bounce 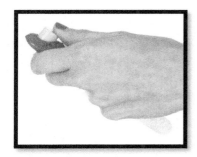 ball scenarios. But remember, never use a clicker without treat because your puppy will start to ignore the clicks. Treats make them feel that they did what was asked and will follow your commands. Give them a treat even if you click by mistake. Wear a treat bag at all times during training so you can click and treat every time your puppy obeys you instantly. It is a good practice to say a word like "Yes" in an upbeat voice at the same moment as you click and treat. The objective is to link in your puppy's brain to the sound of click and the reward. So, every admirable action comes with a click.

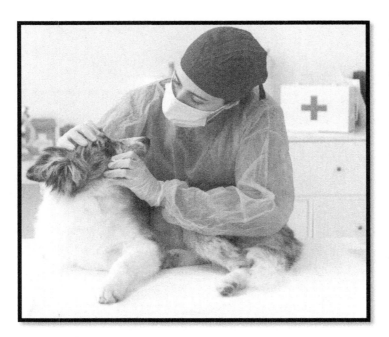

Taking help from a vet

Prepare for the visit beforehand. On the first visit, take all your pet's documents along. Including their vaccinations records, deworming schedule, date of birth, the date you bought or adopted them, microchip number (if any), where they have come from. Take your dog to the vet safely by car or other means of transport. If using a car, sit in the backseat with your dog and both of you wear seatbelts. Bring some cleaning supplies like a towel, cloth, and cleaning solutions just in case the dog gets nervous or carsick. In the waiting room at the vet, keep your dog on a leash and give her some high value treats if she starts to get restless. Vets have some standard procedures for puppies like weighing them on a scale, examining their body parts like ears, eyes, teeth, and arms. They may take a blood sample with a syringe to perform certain tests. It is recommended that you shouldn't stay there during the complicated medical procedures as your puppy might be uncomfortable which would be hard for you to experience. Communicate with the vet properly and express your dog's problem. Follow the medicine or other treatment timetable responsibly. Make a chart or table and mark medicine doses on it (if any).

House Training

You know the place where you live but your new friend doesn't. So, you have to train your puppy to know where to take a bath, where to pee, not to ruin your carpet, where to play and where to rest. This might require a lot of patience on your part but with consistent effort you can train your puppy to become familiar with the house. Your efforts will be worth the reward, a puppy you can truly be proud of.

Receiving Treats Nicely

Puppies are super excited and hyper active beings. Naturally they will receive their favorite treats anxiously and might unintentionally hurt us with their teeth.

You Need

A bag or pouch of low value treats, and an adult around (for the first few times)

Steps

Start in a quiet space with no distraction of sights, smells and sounds.

Keep the treats away so the puppy won't be able to see it or smell it. Take one treat and place it in a closed fist.

Draw attention of your puppy by calling her, taping on the floor, snapping fingers, patting your thigh. If you are in an area with less distractions, then it would be rather easy to draw her attention.

When you make an eye contact, spread out your hand, fist still closed. Take it closer to the puppy's nose as you open your hand. Don't stretch your finger so as to make a cup.

Let her smell it and identify as an edible tasty treat. If you make a cup shape with your hand and it is close enough to her mouth, she wouldn't have to open her mouth completely and you would avoid the accidental bite. She should gently lick it off your hand.

Troubleshooting

If your puppy tries to nibble your closed fist or paws you, then move away your fist and say in upbeat sound 'Oh NO!' to her. Then try again until she is less excited and only smells and licks the treat.

While making a cup with your hand, make sure it's not so stiff as the treat might keep rolling in your palm and fingers, and it should not be too loose that the treat would stick between your fingers.

Potty Training

Potty training is essential for your puppy. If your puppy is healthy, she would follow a schedule that you can note and communicate with everyone around. As you know emergencies can occur, so you have to keep an eye on her. Generally, she would require a trip to her potty spot every hour or two if she is a cute little puppy. Adult dogs have more control and can hold for several hours. A typical schedule would be early morning, afternoon and after dinner or before bedtime. Younger puppies of few months old (3 to 4 months) don't have good bladder control. Smaller dogs also have small bladder. So, you need to keep an eye on them and take them to the 'potty spot' as frequently as possible.

You Need
Walk schedule and potty chart, pen, paper, crate, walking gear (leash, collar, harness), poop bags, potty pads for puppies that are not completely vaccinated, low value treats.

Steps
Get copies of the schedule to record and monitor the whole process. A routine will let you see and know the habit of your puppy.

First early morning trip would be as soon as the puppy wakes up. Take her from crate to the potty spot but don't run as it might excite the puppy and she would 'go' on the way to the spot.

Loosen up the leash and let her sniff the ground now. When she would feel comfortable, she will relieve herself. You should wait patiently during this time as your movement can disturb her natural function. If she doesn't go within 2-3 minutes at the spot then move her few yards away. She will sniff again and might go this time. If for any reason she doesn't go for several minutes, then bring her back and keep an eye on her.

Immediately after her 'business' is over, treat her with low value treats and a lot of praise words. Praise her and give her a value treat immediately so she could connect this reward with her good behavior.

Clean up the poop using poop bags, tie it up and throw it in an outdoor garbage can. This part is hard for some people but when you consider that you want to keep your area clean you will get over it.

Make a note in the schedule right there or when you get back home.

Troubleshooting

Some of the ways in which the puppy is trying to tell you about her bathroom needs; moving into a corner, scratching/standing by the door, circling or pacing, whining, sniffing the ground, coming to you whining or wagging.

She might like to sniff other places on the way but you have to reach the potty spot first.

Attach the leash to the belt if you find it difficult to handle the leash with one hand while scooping the poop. You could also seek help of someone until you get used to it.

Accidents do happen. If your puppy becomes uncontrollable and starts to pee or poo inside, quickly put on a leash and take her out to the potty spot to complete what she started. Praise her outside and give low value treats. If you notice any floor area used as bathroom, don't be angry at the puppy, it will get you nowhere. There is no point showing her the puddle too. The best she could do is to get scared and try to hide the incident even better by choosing more discreet space or even eating it up. If she makes a secret spot inside the house, she would not signal you to take her out to the potty spot. To avoid these drastic results, simply clean the space with an enzymatic cleaner so it would not only be clean but also remove the odor.

If the puppy is not fully vaccinated, you should use potty pads either inside or on a clean pavement. You should, however, use a leash to guide them outside. The puppy must be leashed on each bathroom trip as you want to know their habit and clean up.

Potty Signal

If you have already trained your puppy for potty, she has already learned the basics. She would naturally try to communicate her need when she needs to go potty. You can always be observant but you can't do this all the time. You need to train her to communicate this in an obvious and consistent way.

You need

A hanging strings of bells, basic potty training already done.

Steps

Tie the bell to the door knob that is most commonly used for the exit. If the same door is used by others, mount or tie the bells on the wall besides the door.

Every time you take her out for potty, ring the bell by hand before opening the door, as your puppy watches.

Praise her (even though you have jingled the bell) so that she would associate it with her potty time. When you are back, praise her again. If you do it every time, you will notice that she would start ringing the bell whenever she wants to poop.

Troubleshooting

Don't use any treats for ringing the bell as you don't want her to associate this activity (ringing bell) to food.

Getting along with Crate

A crate or any designated space would be the go-to place for your puppy to have 'me-time'. She should feel safe, secure and undisturbed in her crate. This training can help in many situations such as travelling, gathering at home or repair going on at your place. This can help in potty training too.

As mentioned earlier, you must have selected a place where your puppy will rest and sleep. It could be a crate, kennel or a dog house. In the initial weeks of her arrival, you should train her stay in her crate. Crate is your puppy's private den, don't accompany her there and leave her alone for rest and 'me time'.

You Need
A crate, any worn cloth that smells like you, rubber toy that could be filled with peanut butter or crunchy biscuit, high-value treat, low-value treats

Steps
Stand close to the crate and guide the puppy to the crate. Appreciate when she moves closer to crate and offer a low-value treat. When she gets even closer or sniffs the crate, offer her two low-value treats.

When she enters the crate, offer more praise and low-value treats inside the crate. Keep doing it for every small act she performs to become comfortable in it.

When she is fully inside, offer a high value treat with praise words like, 'Good puppy'.

The puppy might go in and out, offer praise and high-value treat each time she gets in.

When she is settled, give her the rubber toy to play with. Close the door quietly.

After 2-3 minutes open the door quietly and move away. Let her leave the crate whenever she wants as she hasn't learned the 'Stay' command.

If you are using a clicker then you will click when she is inside and having a treat.

Troubleshooting
If your puppy seems anxious or uncomfortable inside the crate, let her out and try again later same day. If she repeats the behavior over the week, then try changing the crate.

Some puppies suffer from separation anxiety even without being restricted. This behavior is damaging to her and your living space. Immediately consult a veterinarian as this situation is beyond your control. Signs of anxiety could be to biting, scratching or pulling the crate bars, shaking, panting, drooling or intense barking.

If your puppy complains by whining or barking when you close the door, let her calm down and stay close to her. If they stop whining, give a high value treat with a gap of a few seconds. Repeat this step three times. Increase the time interval up to 10 minutes gradually. If the puppy still doesn't settle, let her out by a consoling marker 'It's okay', but don't offer a treat.

Never push or pull the puppy into the crate, instead put the chew toy inside the crate to attract her. Your puppy should relate this place with comfort and security. You should not 'ground' your puppy in her crate too as this would create negative connotation for her.

If the puppy had a hard time keeping quiet in her crate, measure the time she kept quiet. Let's say this time was 40 seconds then increase these repetitions to 10 per day and very gradually increase the time.

The puppy should stay less than 4 hours in crate when awake. Only when they sleep this time can be increased, else they would get bored due to lack of activity.

Puppies generally don't use their crates as bathroom. If they do it means they are sick or they are not used to it. You should consult a doctor if they regularly use their crate as washroom. She should feel safe in her crate as the people are around her but not interacting with her.

Responding to names

Giving your puppy a name is very important. It not only brings her closer to you, it also teaches her to respond when you call her and pay attention when you are training her or give her a command. You can choose a name of your choice but it is a good idea to choose one and stick to it (don't try to change it).

You Need:

A small quiet indoor space, a leash and some low value treats, a puppy training clicker (optional) and about 10 minutes of your time.

Steps:

There should not be any distraction in the room especially any sort of noise. Stand close to the puppy with the leash (and clicker if you are using one) in one hand and treat in the other. Don't make an eye contact yet, instead look away.

Say her name in a regular and slightly upbeat tone. She should not feel that you are anxious, angry, in a hurry or frightened. Don't repeat the name over and over. If she doesn't respond, wait a few seconds and then call her name.

When she looks up or ahead and makes eye contact, appreciate her using small praise words like 'good girl', 'nice', 'yes' etc. and then immediately offer one of the treats (and click).

Practice this almost 10 minutes a day with a gap of 20 seconds. When she starts recognizing her name, increase the distance. After some successful attempts try the same exercise in other rooms and outdoors.

Troubleshooting

Sometimes a puppy associates the treat with your hand rather than you calling her name, so she won't make eye contact, instead she would look at your hand with treats expectantly. Don't force them or pull their leash to draw their attention, rather try again and give them time to make eye contact.

Be cool when calling her name, so she would associate it with pleasure and would like her name.

Make a cup with your hand while giving treat to avoid being bitten accidently.

Make sure it's only you in that room other than your puppy. If that isn't possible, at least only one person should be calling her name so she doesn't get confused.

Treat her as soon as she looks at you at name call, don't expect her to come to you or something else. That would be too much for her.

Walk along without pulling leash /
Getting along with leash

The puppies are free spirits. They don't know that pulling a leash could be hazardous for them and their owners and can cause accident. This activity will teach them how to be comfortable with leash and not pull away. You'll start this training at home and then extend it to outdoors.

You Need

Medium length leash (4-6 feet), harness, a handful of treats and any other walking tools you have.

Steps

Clip the leash to the collar. The following instructions are for right-handed people so you can substitute right hand with left if your primary hand is left. Grab the leash with your right hand closer to the puppy and the puppy is on your right. Hold the end of the leash with your left hand. The gap with your right-hand grip and the collar should be enough to make a U shape. It should not be straight or tightened. There should be enough ply for the puppy to move straight without any traction. The extra leash can be wrapped around your left hand so it won't hinder your movement.

Start with a calm standing position and take one step. The puppy should follow without pulling the leash and leash still being loose. Take one step at a time and on every successful step praise the puppy ('good', 'nice', 'yes') and offer a low value treat.

Take about 8-10 steps each day indoors until your puppy can walk 10 steps without stopping or pulling. You should systematically reduce the treat frequency and praise words. Once you feel comfortable taking a walk indoor without you or your puppy pulling the leash, try this outdoors.

Troubleshooting

If your puppy doesn't move or would stretch the leash, don't pull the leash, instead tug once or twice to draw her attention. Don't praise or reward until a task is successful.

Treating immediately will connect her action with reward. You can use the hand closer to the puppy to make her anticipate treat.

If you are using any walking tool like harness, make sure that your puppy is comfortable with it. Let her wear it and play with her while harness is on, so that she won't feel uncomfortable while walking. Similarly leave her for a while in a state wearing collar and leash without anyone controlling her.

In the initial outdoor visits, it is a good idea to have an adult supervise you as the puppy might pull the leash and chase another animal or a vehicle. In later visits you can handle the puppy by yourself.

If your puppy seems distracted or hyper-active, let her drain her energy by having a playtime first.

Living with a pet cat

You Need
A leash, high-value treats, baby gate

Steps
You don't need to introduce the caged pets as they have a different space but a free roaming cat must be introduced to avoid their confrontation. If there's a cat already at home then use a leash even when the puppy enters home for the first time.

She will sniff and identify that there's a cat in the house. She will follow the trail until she finds the cat. The natural response of the puppy is to try to scare the cat away and the cat might run naturally. If the puppy pulls at the leash then pull back and strictly say 'No'. If she responds then praise and give treat.

You can create more than one controlled encounter and repeat the desired behavior. Alternatively, you can use a baby gate separate space for both pets.

Troubleshooting
Always give space to the cat to flee so they feel free.

Don't let your puppy chase the cat.

Small caged pets should not be taken out of cage in presence of your puppy.

Living with another puppy

Steps
Let both of the puppies outside home until they become comfortable with each other. See the section socialization for more details. Two household members should walk the two puppies independently at the same park. Observe their behavior and wait until they get along.

Troubleshooting
It might take a while for two pets to get along with each other. Make sure you are present on each encounter.

Visiting Vet and Groomer
This activity will prepare your puppy for stay calm and feel safe on her visit to vet or groomer.

You Need
Metal spoon, towel, different grooming brushes/gloves, dog toothbrush, high-value treats

Steps
When your puppy is relaxing or playing with you, pat and scratch her back, sides, neck, head, forehead, tail, paw and lower jaw. With certain type of touch the puppy might not be comfortable but when she allows you to touch, say approval marker ('Yes', 'Good', 'Nice') to her and treat her. You should go slow and do this a few minutes a day.

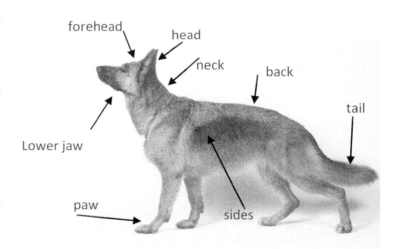

When the puppy becomes familiar with your touch (patting, massaging and cuddling) then use different objects like massaging with towel, brushing with a brush or glove, for a few minutes a day. Softly rub the dog tooth brush around the muzzle avoiding the eyes. Use a metal spoon to probe the chest and belly area as if it were stethoscope. Every time your puppy lets you interact with a new object, praise and give her high-value treat.

Finally, after several days when the puppy is calm, start cupping her paw in your hand gently. At the final stage you might want to touch her muzzle to brush her teeth. There must be an adult in this last part and only with their consultation you should proceed.

Troubleshooting
If your puppy is excited and playful, let her play until she is not that active. This should be done before taking her to the vet or a groomer.

Watch the body language of the puppy; if her eyes seem larger than usual, she's yawning or has her tail tucked between her legs or growling, stop and take a break until she gets back to normal.

Never force a touch when your puppy is not ready otherwise, she might be offended and bite to convey her discomfort.

For the muzzle part of activity, you can apply peanut butter or high-value treat inside her mouth.

Stop unnecessary barking at the door

Since your puppy can't talk, we have limited ways of communicating with each other. Barking could be a powerful communication tool but only if your puppy doesn't always bark in every situation. Another offshoot of barking is that it will keep the puppy constantly excited, which is not good for her. So, in this activity we'll teach her to divert her attention from the scenarios which are unusual for her but might be normal for us.

You Need
Some high-value treats, a leash, a human partner, the 'Sit' command.

Steps
It is normal for your puppy to bark when anyone familiar enters the house or the yard. This is their way of welcoming excitedly. So first, go outside and come back after 2-3 minutes. Make sure you have some treats with you to offer her upon your return.

When you return and hear her barking, do not enter until the barking stops.

Reward her with a treat and say 'Quiet Down' in an upbeat but calm voice. Give her a simple command such as 'Sit' so that her attention is diverted.

Keep practicing over short intervals then increase the gap from few minutes to 15, 25 minutes and eventually an hour or more. Every household member should participate in this activity as it is natural.

Stop barking at the strangers

Steps
Attach a leash when the delivery person arrives at the door or any other stranger. Your puppy will recognize them from a distinct smell.

When your puppy starts barking when someone approaches the door, walk calmly to your puppy

with a treat in your hand. Get the puppy's attention by calling her name and say the command word 'Quiet Down' or 'Quiet Now'. This way she will be notified that you have noticed her signal. If she does stop, treat her.

Hook the leash to her and then walk her away from the door to her crate. Give them a simple command like 'Stay' or 'Sit' and reward them with praise. Meanwhile someone else can answer the door.

Troubleshooting
Be patient. Don't shout at them the command words like 'Quiet Now'. Raising your voice will give your puppy the signal that YOU are excited or nervous just like her. She will continue barking more rigorously.

If the puppy steps back while barking or show any other sign that she is frightened, let an adult take care of her and answer the door yourself.

Meeting other dogs and puppies

Dogs are tribal animal and they try to protect their tribe. Their tribe is whom they live with and in case of your puppies you and people around you, is their tribe. Initially, your puppy would be scared or aggressive towards stranger animals. Teaching your puppy to get along well with other dogs can lead to friendships and fun games.

You Need
A leash, high-value treats, a friend with a dog, an adult to supervise, a neutral ground (anywhere neither of the dogs would associate with themselves)

Steps
Have an adult make an appointment with a friend at a park or an open space. It's not a good idea to meet at home or yard where either of the dogs are 'living'. The clan approach will make her possessive and protective towards her clan.

Walk the puppy about 10-20 feet away from each other. Walk in the same direction but don't let them interact as of yet. If your puppy remains calm and composed in other dog's presence or show interest in meeting them, give her a treat and praise her.

As long as she is comfortable, gradually take her closer. If she shows signs of defensive behavior, increase the distance. Defensive behavior signs include; hair standing on the back, teeth-baring, growling.

Let both of the dogs decide how much time they would take to get comfortable with each other. If they get along well in the first meeting then start walking in the same direction. Still keep an eye on your puppy and see if she behaves strangely.

After several such encounters, an adult can decide that they are ready to meet off-leash. Let them meet in a closed space and make sure there is no common interest object like treats or toys so they won't fight over it.

Troubleshooting

Don't rush as it can damage the relationship for good. Once your puppy associates the other puppy with fear or anger, it would be hard to reset the feeling. Realize that both of the dogs would be anxious and they need ample time to get to know each other.

We recognize people from their faces and dogs remember people with their smell. So, if the dogs try to smell every part of the other dog, that's perfectly fine. Think of it, as their way of saying hello to each other and remembering their faces and names.

Don't force them to get along, they would or they won't.

You and your friend, both should hold the leash firmly even if the dogs like each other. The puppies can be excited to meet each other and can get out of control.

If a fight breaks out between dogs, don't intervene, instead, ask an adult for help. The excited, stressed or scared dog can unwillingly bite you, even if they don't mean to.

Obedience training

In this section we will make connections in the puppy's brain. We will relate the common actions such as sleep, stop, leave etc. with the command words and possibly a hand gesture. This is an extremely powerful way to bond with your pet and let her show that how much she cares by following your orders.

Touch

This command is an easy way to build trust with your puppy. She would learn that your hand or any object you offer, is safe to touch. This also lets her focus on one object at a time. This skill will be useful in more exciting activities.

You Need

A small, quiet room with no distractions, a leash (to practice outside), pouch of low value dry treats

Steps

 Keep the treat in a closed fist and hide it behind your back. Extend the other hand with open palm, slowly in front of your puppy. Let her explore your hand by sniffing and then touching with her nose. When they do, encourage her with praise words like 'good', 'nice' and treat them.

Now switch hands and repeat the previous step 10 times with an interval of a few seconds. If your puppy is having a hard time doing it, take a break.

In this step we will link the command word 'Touch' with the action already known to her. Offer your empty, open hand and say in loud and positive tone 'Touch'. Praise and reward with a treat.

Repeat the previous step 10 times. Practice this every day. Then try this in different indoor spaces. Gradually increase the distance and finally try this outdoors. Always use a leash when you are outside. When she responds even from a short distance without distraction, she's learnt the command.

Troubleshooting

If you have a very shy puppy, then first use your spread-out hand with palm facing down. Next try to stand with your body facing away from her. You want to make it as non-threatening as possible.

You can even lower the tone of command word 'Touch'. Finally, you can replace the low value treats with high value ones.

If your puppy is too young and would try to chew your hand rather than touching it, try the 'Taking the Treats Gently' activity first.

Keep the treat hand hidden until she has completed the task so that she would focus on the command instead of treats.

Sit

This powerful command teaches your puppy self-discipline. She will greet people and wait for further instructions patiently. She will learn that no matter how excited she is, she won't get a treat until she sits patiently.

You Need

Quiet place with no distraction, high-value treat

Steps

Grab a treat in your hand and make a fist with the treat inside it. Let your puppy smell it so she knows you have a treat for her.

Slowly move the hand upwards without touching her. Don't open your hand as yet. When it is above her height, make sure she is almost sitting.

When she sits back without jumping to get the treat, praise her and give her the treat. Practice this a couple of times in a row until she sits down without difficulty.

Finally, add the command word 'Sit' with the previous step. The command should be given in clear, consistent and strong voice. Praise and treat her when she follows the order. Repeat 5 times in a row until she gets it. Gradually you will reduce the treat frequency, until you are able to just say the word (with a hand gesture) and she follows it even without a treat. You can use praise words though.

Troubleshooting

The distance of your treat hand with respect to her eyes and nose is critical. If you place your hand too close to her, she would move backwards rather than sitting to get a better look at it. If you raise your hand too high (above her eyebrow level) then she might try to jump towards it.

It is relatively harder to make your puppy sit when she is excited. Let's say she sees you after a while, she would like to jump over you, rub against you to show her eagerness. When she does that turn your body away and stand firm. Ignore her until she is calm. Tell her to 'Sit' and reward her with chin scratching and patting only when she has all her four paws on the floor.

Young puppies have hard time sitting, they might slip trying to do so. You can either help her sit by scooping her back and lifting her chest. You can also try this activity standing next to wall so that she could take the support of the wall while sitting and would not slip.

Check

This command helps your puppy concentrate and create a strong bond. Locking gaze in animal world means to weigh the strenght of the other party to fight. This also serves the purpose of intimidating the other. With this command you teach them to look into the eye without intimidation. You can quickly draw attention of your puppy, build connection and help her focus on the path in busy streets.

You Need

Low-value treats, 'Sit' and 'Wait' commands and good self-control.

Steps

Sit in front of your puppy and order them to 'Sit'. Hold a treat in your fist and let her smell it.

Raise your treat hand up to your nose between your eyes. When she looks into your eyes, lock the gaze as long as you can. Praise and give her the treat. Repeat this exercise 10 times in a row.

Hold the treat hand behind your back and use empty hand to point at your nose and say 'Check'. If she makes an eye contact and is not searching for or looking around the treat, appreciate her with 'Good', 'Nice' or 'Yes'. Give the treat. Repeat this activity 10 times in a row.

Repeat the previous step but increase the duration of eye contact. Count to three to hold the gaze for 3 seconds and then give the praise her and give her the treat. Gradually increase the time and take it up to 5 seconds.

Now you want her to 'Check' in the outdoor setting. You need to use 'Check' with the leash on and while walking indoor. Try this activity in the kitchen where there could be a lot of distraction.

Troubleshooting

If the puppy doesn't pay attention to you with the treat hand behind, then first call her name and then say 'Check'.

If the puppy doesn't have self-control and has not learnt the 'Wait' command, she might jump at you when you show your treat hand close to your face. Don't try this if she is excited or have not learnt to stay calm.

Heel

This command teaches your puppy to stay close to you while walking and standing. She will learn to stay slightly behind you and not walk in zigzag or walk ahead of you. You will try this activity only when the puppy is comfortable walking with a leash.

You Need

Low-value treats, walking gear, 'Touch' and 'Check' already learnt

Steps

Start with a quiet isolated space. Use the proper leash grab position and keep the treats away from the puppy.

Walk a few steps maintaining the distance with the puppy, if she pulls the leash or tries to walk ahead of you, stop.

Say the command word 'Check' to draw attention of your puppy. Drop your hand to the knee level as if you are offering it to 'Touch' but don't say the command word 'Touch'.

When the puppy adjusts her position, behind you and close to you, say the word 'Heel' and offer treat with the hand close to your knee.

Repeat the previous step until you could take 4 steps with your puppy next to you. When she heels, encourage her with praise words and multiple treats. Repeat the steps, increasing the number of steps before the treat.

Offer more treats or praises when the puppy 'Heel' quicker.

Troubleshooting

If your puppy is shy and keeps a distance from you while waking, use high-value treats, walk at a slower pace to match her speed and be patient.

Down

This command will teach your puppy to lie down in resting position with their fore-legs spread out. This makes her less excitable and gives her time to relax. It alsoimproves her focus.

You Need

High-value treats in each hand, a soft spot for them to lie down (a blanket, towel, grassy patch etc.), the 'Sit' command and know how to take treats gently.

Steps

Put a towel or blanket on the floor. Grab the high-value treat in both hands, stand next to the cloth and hide one of the hands behind your back. Use the other hand to attract the puppy to come to the cloth piece.

Tell her to 'Sit' on the blanket. As she sits, you kneel in front of her to get to her eye level.

Just like 'Sit' lure her to look and smell the treat from appropriate distance. Now lower your hand in straight line so she is in a lying position. When she successfully lays down, praise her and reward her from the hand behind not the one you used for luring.

Now repeat the exercise with the commad word 'Down'. Gradually increase the time before rewarding, use more encouragement and affection rathar than treats. Start giving this command without a treat in hand and without lowering all the way down. She will start to recognize the keyword and your gesture to her action.

Troubleshooting

It is recommended to teach 'Down' after 'Sit', this way you could use far less treats and praise more often. Sometimes puppies stand or sit right after the 'Down' position. You can praise and treat them when you casually ask them to 'Down', but during the training make sure you reward them when they stay in that position.

When practicing in different places or surfaces, you might need the same piece of cloth that you started the practice with. First attempt would be on the same blanket and then gradually remove it in subsequent practice.

If the puppy is lowering down only the front of her body and not the back, you could ask someone to help her lay down. They can gently push her backside to lower or scoop to make her proper 'Down' position. Don't treat her until she is in the correct position.

Drop It

This command lets your puppy let go of anything she is holding in her mouth. This is very important command as we don't have to remove the object manually as she has a tight grab. Similarly if she is holding onto something which is not good for her, we can quickly instruct her to let go. This will also come in handy for more advanced tricks.

You Need

A low-value toy or item, a high-value toy or item, high-value treat for advanced steps.

Steps

Using a toy, play with your puppy for about 10 to 20 seconds. Wrap your hands around part of toy so that she can't put the whole toy in her mouth.

Stop playing and hold on to the toy until she gets bored and let go of it, praise her right there. Play again and repeat a few times.

Play again and this time, the moment she leaves the toy, say 'Drop It'. When she looks at you, praise her. Repeat this activity 10 times.

Hold the toy with less portion in your hand and repeat the exercise. With practice you would be able to ask the item to 'Drop It' even if you are not holding it.

Try this after successfully teaching 'Drop It'.

Hold a high-value treat in a fist and let your puppy smell and sniff your hand.

Say the command word 'Drop It' as she opens the mouth to release the object, give her high value treat and remove the forbidden object with the other hand.

Troubleshooting

Sometimes your puppy might change the game and runs away with the toy. Don't chase it, rather increase the treat value to convince her to 'Drop It'.

This activity should be performed by an adult whom your puppy trusts as taking an object from her could be challenging. Alternatively, choose a very high-value treat to make it work.

If the puppy shows any of these signs, call an adult; growling, looking at you sideways and angrily, stiffening of body or hair standing.

Off

This command teaches the good behavior of not getting too excited and jumping on people or objects. This action can break the objects and trip or scare people. Timing is important as you have to behave quickly and catch the puppy 'in action' to tell her that this behavior is not acceptable. This requires a lot of effort and patience as we are reprogramming their instinct behavior, but once learnt, the puppy will have a decent behavior in the future.

You Need

High-value treat (easily accessible to you but far from the puppy), 'Sit' command

Steps

While you are observing your puppy casually, notice when she put her forelegs on an object with an intention to jump further. You will say the command 'Off' to let her know this is unacceptable behavior. Say it in a serious, stern and positive voice. Your tone should not be shrill or scolding or yelling as this might be interpreted wrongly by her.

Quickly grab the treat and praise her of her good behavior then offer her a treat.

Troubleshooting

Consistency is the key. Spread the word among everyone in the house so whenever she tries to climb or jump over a piece of furniture, she gets the same treatment. When your puppy jumps over, some people might find it cute and allow this behavior, but you have to be consistent and tell them that you are training your pup and call her 'Off'.

You can attach a leash to let her off of that object but don't offer a treat in this case.

Puppies are clever, if your puppy realizes that you treat her as soon as she is about to jump or gets over a forbidden object, she might deliberately perform this action. In this case follow the 'Off' command with 'Sit' and then praise and reward her.

Wait

This is a command to teach your puppy to be patient and show good manners. She should wait for the treat or next instruction with all paws on the floor. She should be relatively calm and not moving anxiously.

You Need

Low-value treats, high-value treats, a favorite toy, food dish with small puppy food portion (at mealtime), 'Off' command

Steps

When your puppy is still, sitting or standing, fist a low-value treat behind your back and then slowly extend your hand at shoulder level.

Now lower your fist to her nose level. This action should take about 5 seconds.

If she jumps at it before you lower your hand, say 'Off' and start over when her all four paws are back on the floor

When she is waiting patiently, treat her and praise her. Gradually increase the time to 10 seconds. The aim is 15 seconds.

Do this a few times. Stop this activity if your puppy is distracted or bored. Once learnt you can apply the same activity for food, high-value treat and toy. Remember to always praise her desirable actions.

Troubleshooting

If the 'Off' command doesn't work the first time, turn your body away from her and don't pay attention to them until she calms down.

If your puppy is too small, then kneel instead of standing for this activity. Additionally, you could start the activity at waist height rather than shoulder height.

Place

This command works like 'Stay' but with a specified location. This is useful when you go to a place and you designate a spot for your puppy. She will think that it is safe to 'Stay' at that particular location. It is also useful when people are coming and going (like a party) so the puppy would stay at specific place.

Same picture as illustration with a blanket or bed underneath

You Need

A leash, blanket or puppy bed, high-value treats

'Touch', 'Down', 'Stay' and 'Responding to name' activity should be taught first

Steps

Use a leash even indoor for activity. You don't need to hold the leash but you might if the puppy deviates from the command.

Setup her resting place by laying bed or blanket as she watches you do that. She might come closer to you. If she doesn't, you can use a treat to call her closer.

As she steps on the blanket or bed, praise her and give her the treat. You can use the 'Touch' command by placing your empty hand on the blanket and giving her the treat when she gets on the blanket. Walk her away from the spot. Repeat this exercise and increase the number of treats as she puts in more paws on the blanket and when she stays longer. This way she would associate the reward (treats) with two actions; stepping on a specific spot and staying longer.

Once she gets on the blanket with all paws on it, give 'Down' and then 'Stay' command. Treat and praise her on both steps separately.

When she is following the sequence of previous steps consistently, it's time to add the 'Place' command. Stand next to blanket or puppy bed and call her pointing towards the bed. When she pays attention to you after responding to her name, she might initially get confused. Give her a few seconds to respond to 'Place' command. If she successfully walks to the bed, lays down and stays there, praise and treat her. After 5 successful repetitions you can increase the distance between you and the bed.

Troubleshooting

Remember to praise and reward the puppy when they complete all the steps.

If the puppy quickly gets back from the 'Stay', give her a chew toy so she could stay longer.

The chew toy is particularly useful for younger puppies that are teething. Use a worn t-shirt or worn-out towel as they might be tempted to chew their soft bed or fluffy blanket. Once they receive the chew toy, they would stay longer and avoid chewing at the blanket.

If during the activity, she goes too far away from you or the 'Place', you can use the leash and walk her back. Once she is trained, you can remove the leash. Use the leash when practicing outside until she recognizes her name so well that she would return to you upon hearing her name, regardless of the distractions around.

Stay

This is a powerful command that lets your puppy stay in one place for a longer period of time. This is not only slightly challenging but also a more rewarding activity. You don't have to keep her bound to you, instead you can move about and take her along whenever you wish. To teach 'Stay' command, we would break it down into smaller objective. First objective is to make her stay and then increase the distance between you and the puppy. The second objective is to increase the duration. The final objective is that she does that in the presense of distractions.

You Need

High-value treats, 'Sit' command

Steps

Stand close to the puppy and ask her to 'Sit'. When she is sitting, praise and reward her. Now perform a hand gesture to stop and give the command 'Stay'. Palm facing towards the puppy, fingers joined and thumb in front of the chest.

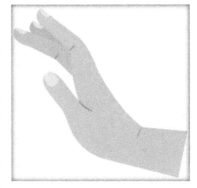

Look up and straight beyond your puppy, without making eye contact, take a step back. You should wait for about 5 seconds before going to next step.

Now get back to your original position (take a step forward) still not making eye contact. If she maintains her position, make eye contact, praise and reward her. Gradually increase the distance up to 5 steps but keep the time interval to 5 seconds.

Repeat the previous instructions following the same 1 to 5 steps increments but wait for 10 seconds on each step back. She deserves two treats now as she has increased the distance and time to 'Stay' without you making eye contact. For 15 seconds make it 3 treats one after another. With 5 seconds interval take it to 30 seconds where you give her loads of praises, affection and 5 treats. Make sure now you can practice this 5 times in a row.

The final step in 'Stay' is to add a distraction. You would move but your puppy won't. Imagine your puppy is in the center of a circle and you step sideways maintaining the distance. When stepping sideways, you'd be circling around your puppy but she should 'Stay' in her position. If she gets up, ask her to 'Sit'. Take one step at a time.

Slowly take 3 steps towards your right, wait for 5 seconds and then traceback 1 step and wait for 5 seconds.

Move back to your original position (5 steps away from her, facing her) and praise them to let them know this part of exercise is over. Give her up to 3 treats. Continue this exercise if your puppy is not exhausted or bored. Move up to 5 steps.

Once you could make a semi-circle 5 times in a row, start circling without stopping or looking at her. If she 'Sit' and 'Stay' without looking at you or repositioning herself, then praise her and give 5 treats. Try doing the full circle 5 times in a row.

Troubleshooting

Once practiced enough, try making variations like making an outward spiral, i.e. moving away from her while making a circle. If she stays without you in her line of sight, that is an achievement.

Do not make eye contact until you have completed one set of steps and it's time to reward her. When you make eye contact, she might think she is free to go. Remember to use praise words before giving treat so she would know what is expected of her.

When you take her out for 'Stay', initially take her to an outside enclosed space. Use a longer leash to help her focus on the activity.

Leave It

This command is to keep your puppy away from harmful food items such as poisionous and choking items. This will greatly reduce the emergency situation as you train her not to eat or chew anything that is not good for her.

You Need
Low-value treats, high-value treats, 'Wait'

Steps
Grab a high-value treat in one hand and a low value treat in another. Hide the high-value treat behind your back.

Kneel and extend your fist with low-value treat in it. Your puppy will explore it by sniffing or pawing. The moment she looks away from the fist, praise her and reward her with high-value treat. Repeat 5 times in a row before moving on.

Add the command 'Leave It' when she begins to show interest in your low-value treat fist. Say the command word before she sniffs or paws. If she looks at you or looks away from the fist, praise her and reward her with high-value treat.

The last part is tricky for you and tough for her. This time lay your low-value treat hand on the floor with palm up and treat visible. As soon as she notices the treat say the command word. If she follows your command and looks away or at you, praise and treat her. If she ignores your verbal command or gets too close to claim the treat, close your fist, put it behind your back and start over.

It's time to raise the bar. Let an adult supervise this part. Place the treat on the floor and be ready to cover it with your hand quickly. Sit in front of your puppy, place the treat on the floor closer to you and say 'Leave It'. If she still tries to claim the treat, cover it with your hand and give disapproving marker 'No, No' or 'O Oh'. Don't push her away. If she follows your command give her multiple high-value treats and lots of praises and affection.

Repeat the previous step and gradually move the treat closer to her until you place it between her forelegs and she doesn't take it following your verbal command 'Leave It'.

Now let's add some more distraction through movement. Toss a low value treat closer to you and away from her. Before the treat lands say 'Leave It'. If the puppy moves towards it, disregarding your command then cover the treat and show disapproval. You can practice 'Leave It' with 'Wait command. If you live in an urban area, then she needs extensive training on this. Keep plenty of high value treats ready when you walk her in the city. She will be overwhelmed with the sights and smells of objects around her. Every time she obeys your command give her high-value treat.

Troubleshooting

The objective of 'Leave It' is to have your puppy ignore food laying on the floor or sidewalk. So don't leave the low-value treat on the floor and don't let them eat it off the floor even after the activity. Remove the treats if she shows interest in eating them and distract her with a chew toy or another activity.

You can try 'Leave It' command for really young puppies when the try to chew objects like shoes, carpet, curtain etc.

You can use the help of an adult in covering the treat. You should not move too quickly or seem excited as the puppy might think we are playing a game and would try to outsmart you in speed.

Cool Tricks

These commands are not essential but are neat. You could show off to your friends and brag about the abilities of your puppy. Dogs are intelligent and active beings, always willing to learn new things. Teaching extra tricks can help the dog stay busy. You can choose which of these tricks you want her to learn. You should not overwhelm your puppy with these commands until she has mastered the basics and is consistent.

Take It

This command will tell your puppy to hold onto an object in her mouth for a longer time. This skill will help in playing fetch.

You Need

low-value treats, high-value treats, a low-value toy.

Steps

Kneel down near your puppy on the floor and place the toy on the ground. The moment your puppy touches the toy with their mouth, praise and give them a low value teat. Pick the toy up and put down a moment later. Repeat the process about five times.

The final goal for this exercise is to have your puppy hold the toy in their mouth for a long time. After your puppy touches the toy with their mouth five times, you should advance, and reward them when they can pick it up with their mouth. After they pick it up five times. You should increase the time they need to hold it in their mouth to get a treat. The longer they hold it, the more treats they should get.

Once your puppy seems comfortable in picking up a toy and holding it in their mouth for 15 seconds, teach them to take the toy from your hand instead of the floor. Repeat the first two steps with the toy in your hand. Teach them to recognize that you are encouraging them to take the toy from your hand.

When your dog is able to take the toy from your hand ten times consecutively, start saying the verbal command 'Take It' before they take the toy.

Next you can switch the low value toy with a high value one. Also, try this exercise with other different objects. Don't use any objects that can be too heavy for them, or are so small they might swallow, and things with smooth surfaces which might be hard to hold in their teeth.

Troubleshooting

If your dog seems unable to hold the object for a long time, check if the object is a suitable size. Use a smaller and/or lighter object for instance. Use high value toys for dogs who need extra encouragement and are not very active with low value toys.

If your dog doesn't let go of an item they are holding in their mouth, never force it out, instead offer them something else, such as a treat.

If your dog doesn't hold something in their mouth, don't try to force them. This can confuse them or at its worst, frighten them.

Leap

Your puppy will learn how to leap over a stick, a hula hoop or another object.

You Need

High-value treats, a large room or a yard with ample space, a stick, 2 blocks of wood or 2 stacks of books.

Steps

Place a stick while your puppy is sitting on one side of the stick and you on the other side. Make a fist with high-value treat and let her sniff it. Move your hand down and take it closer to the stick.

When the fist is at your puppy's eye level, contract your hand and let her follow the cue. Reward her with a treat and praise words when she walks over the stick. Repeat a few times.

Now add a book on both sides of the stick. This will make an obstacle for her but she should be able to comfortably cross over it. This time using the same method, say the command word 'Leap'. Repeat these steps 5 to 10 times.

When your puppy learns to 'Leap' over the stick, increase the height ever so slightly. With practice, you can make them jump through a hula hoop, the height of their eye level.

Troubleshooting

If your puppy tries to walk around the stick instead of jumping, guide them back and check the height of stick and lower it.

Your puppy is not going for Olympics. Don't make it hard for her. It should be a game that both of you enjoy. Not all puppies have the same energy level or jumping capabilities.

Crawl

Your puppy will learn to crawl across the carpet or grass.

You Need

High-value treats, a carpeted room or a grassy patch, 'Down' command.

Steps

Start in the 'Down' position. Place the high-value treat in a closed fist and let her sniff it.

Lower your fist and put it on the floor in front of her. Now retreat your hand, still on the floor, a few inches away from her. If she follows without getting up, praise and reward her. If she rises up, ask her to lie 'Down' again. Don't reward until she crawls to the treat. Repeat this a few times.

Now add the command 'Crawl' as you move the treat away from her. Repeat this until she gets hold of the command and its associate action.

Finally increase the distance and don't drag your fist on the floor, instead just place your hand on the floor and say 'Crawl'. If she moves towards the treat without rising up, appreciate, praise and give her treat. Repeat this a few times.

Troubleshooting

If your puppy gets up rather than crawling, she might need more practice with 'Down'. If she gets up in 3rd or 4th step, then increase the distance slowly.

Make sure this activity is performed on a soft surface such as carpet or grass. Hard surface will not only be difficult but also painful for your puppy.

Tunnel

Your puppy will learn to walk through a tunnel.

You Need

High-value treats, 'Sit' and 'Stay' commands.

Steps

Start by saying 'Sit' and 'Stay'. Grab a high-value treat and let her sniff it.

Facing her, increase the distance between your legs.

Hold the treat behind the 'tunnel' made with your legs. Say the command 'Tunnel' and move your hand away so she has to walk through the 'tunnel' to get to the treat. When she follows your command, praise and reward her.

You can make variation like asking them to walk under a chair to reach you. Later you can also add cloth to the side of the chair to make it more like a tunnel.

Troubleshooting
Your puppy might be reluctant at first to move underneath your legs, but with lot of patience, encouragement and practice she can learn it.

Keep your balance as your puppy might bump into your legs while passing through, so stand firm.

Get Excited
This will train your puppy to experess her happiness and excitement.

You Need
High-value treats, 'Sit' and 'Place' commands.

Steps
Stand in front of your puppy while she is also standing. Grab a high-value treat and let her sniff it off of your fist.

Maintaining a distance from your puppy, walk in a circle as your puppy follows you. You should walk at a medium pace as if you move too fast, your puppy might not complete the circular movement and if you are too slow, she might not get that it was a circular motion. When you complete a circle, reward her. Repeat this a few times.

Now raise your hand just above your puppy's head and make a large circular motion. She will still follow and jitter a bit. Make two circles before praising and treating her.

Now grab a treat and hide it from her. Use your empty hand to make a circle and add the command, 'Get Excited'. If she makes two full circles while jumping with joy, praise her and treat her.

Troubleshooting
If your puppy likes this movement and 'dances around' without the command, don't pay attention to it. Instead ask her to 'Sit' or 'Place' and reward for siting.

Make sure you don't hold the treat hand too high as the puppy might think that it's a game of jumping at the treat and would not move in a circle.

Rest

Teach your puppy to rest their chin on your lap. It is a polite way to greet somone they love.

A kid sitting on the floor with legs spread out, the puppy resting her chin on their thigh across.

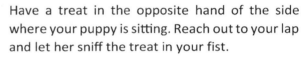

You Need

High-value treats, 'Down' command.

Steps

Sit on the floor with your legs straight out in front of you. Call your dog and ask them to 'Down' next to you.

Have a treat in the opposite hand of the side where your puppy is sitting. Reach out to your lap and let her sniff the treat in your fist.

Slowly lure her so her chin is resting on your thigh.

Wait for two seconds in this position and then praise and treat her. Do this 10 times in a row before moving on to the next step.

Now add the verbal command 'Rest'. When she does, reward her with praise and a treat.

Practice this daily for about a week. Once she learns the command, say it without luring her. You can pat on your thigh and ask her to 'Rest'. Only reward when she places her chin for a few seconds.

Troubleshooting

Increase the time she stays in 'Rest' position slowly.

If the puppy gets too excited with the treat and jumps over your leg to receive the treat, use low-value treats.

Bow

Bow is a signal for playtime.

You Need

High-value treats

Steps

Get into crouching position in front of your puppy. Then extend your forearms and rise your back for a brief moment. If she copies with same movement, immediately praise her and give her a treat. Repeat until she does this every time you do it.

Now add the 'Bow' command as you get into this position. Praise and reward for desired response. Repeat a few times.

With daily practice, she should be able to 'Bow' on your verbal command and you no longer have to bow yourself.

Troubleshooting

Don't get too close to the puppy and give her ample space so she won't think you're about to attack.

If your puppy gives you hard time getting this one right, catch her in the act of stretching. Say the command 'Bow' and when she stretches like this, praise and treat her.

Paw

This command will teach your puppy to offer her paw for handshake. This activity will help her prepare her for vet or groomer visits in the future.

You Need

High value treats, 'Sit' command.

Steps

Grab the treat in a fist, get close to the puppy and ask her to 'Sit'.

Move your treat hand to the side of her muzzle and move down your hand slowly towards her paw. Make sure she doesn't follow your hand with her nose, if she does, start over.

When your treat hand is close to her paw, she might try to open it with her paw. When her paw touches your hand, praise and treat her.

Practice this until she lifts her paw, when she does, say 'Paw' and when the paw touches your hand, praise and reward her.

When your puppy learns to 'Paw' with treat, practice with palm open and the command word 'Paw. If she responds', reward her with praise and affection.

Troubleshooting
If your puppy doesn't lift the paw at all, guide her paw gently with your hand and say the command word.

Never squeeze the paw as the dogs are very sensitive about their paws.

Bring It
This useful command lets your puppy pick an item and bring it back to you.

You Need
Low-value treats, a dog toy or any lightweight object, another person to help you, 'Take It' and 'Drop It' commands and knowing their name.

Steps
Sit in front of your puppy and ask your helper to sit a few yards away from you with a treat on them.

Hold the toy in your hand and say 'Take It'. Let her hold the object for a few seconds but don't reward her as yet.

Let your helper call your puppy and after getting her attention say the command 'Bring It'. The helper should have one or both hands spread towards the puppy with palms up.

When the puppy reaches the helper, put the open palm under the toy and say 'Drop It'. Even if she drops it near your helper, you can still praise and treat her as she has combined the tasks of 'Take It', 'Bring It' and 'Drop It'.

Switch places with your helper and repeat the exercise for a few minutes.

At the final stage, place the toy on the floor and ask her to 'Take It'. Move away and ask her to 'Bring It'. When she gets to you, ask her to 'Drop It'. Reward her with praises and treat. Once she can perform this trick only with your help, you can change objects, increase distance and change surroundings.

Troubleshooting

Don't reward her if she doesn't bring the toy to your helper, instead help her by cheering and encouraging with positive words. If she drops halfway through, try to decrease the distance.

If your pup feels bored by fetching the same toy over and over, use 4 toys and exchange them one by one.

If your puppy shows possessive behavior and runs away with the toy, don't chase or try to snatch the toy, instead use another less attractive toy or object next time.

High Five

Your best buddy will learn to give you a high five.

You Need

High-value treats, 'Sit' and 'Paw' commands

Steps

Sit in front of your puppy and grab a treat in your fist.

Start with the 'Paw' motion but as she lifts her paw, open your hand with palm facing her. You want the puppy to touch your palm with her paw.

Practice this for a while until she learns to touch your palm with her paw. Now raise your hand in front of her chest and say 'High Five'. When she gives you a high five, praise her and treat her.

Keep practicing and keep increasing the distance of your palm from her chest. Don't make it uncomfortable for your puppy though.

Troubleshooting

Sometimes your open palm gesture might be confused by your puppy as 'Touch' and she will try to sniff or touch with the muzzle rather than her paw. Don't reward her for this and start over.

Don't grab her paw, just let her tap gently.

When practicing with distance, she might like jumping and giving you a high five with force. Wear a sock on your hand to avoid any scratches. Treat and appreciate her only when she gently taps.

Play Dead

Your drop-dead gorgeous puppy will perform the dropping dead act.

You Need

High-value treats, soft spot (carpeted or grassy patch), 'Down' and 'Roll Over' commands.

Steps

Choose a soft surface like carpet or grass. Hold the treat by the side of your puppy's head close to her muzzle. Slowly move in an even curved motion to the floor. Keep your hand close to the muzzle. Once she lies down on the floor, praise and treat her. Repeat this activity a few times.

Once she gets hold of the movement, add the command word 'Play Dead' and move your hand a little faster. Praise and treat her. Repeat this about 5 more times.

Say the command without hand movement and finally increase the distance.

Troubleshooting

If she does 'Roll Over' instead of 'Play Dead', try again. It might take a few days before she fully understands what is your intention.

Don't push or pull the puppy to the side, let her figure out how to naturally lay on her side.

Speak

In the beginning we taught our puppy to stop barking unnecessarily. In this act she will bark on our command. For young puppies this is cute and when she gets older you can use this command to know where she is right now.

You Need
High-value treats, 'Sit' command

Steps
Grab a high value treat in your fist and let her smell it.

Ask her to 'Sit' so she won't be over excited.

Now say her name and ask her to 'Speak'. If she makes only eye contact in response to her name but doesn't bark, you can encourage her by barking at her. Once she gets what to do, she might get up and bark. It's fine as long as she makes some noise. Repeat a few times.

When she consistently makes noise on your 'Speak' command, reduce the frequency of treat to full barks only.

Troubleshooting
If your puppy just stands up or misunderstands your command and tries to do some other trick, give her disapproval signal politely like 'uh Oh'. Start over from the 'Sit' command.

As mentioned earlier this might be confusing for a puppy to see disapproval for unnecessary barking and approval for instructed barking. Be patient, she will pick up the difference and bark only at command.

If your puppy gets super excited and does other tricks along with barking, ignore her and show disapproval. Try it some other time of the day when she is not so active.

Shame

Teach your puppy to act ashamed by brushing her paws with her muzzle.

You Need

Low-value treats, tape or sticky notes, 'Sit' or 'Down' command

Steps

Start with your puppy in 'Sit' or 'Down' position.

Place a sticky note on her nose, when she tries to remove it with her paw, praise her and treat her. Repeat this a few times.

Now add the command word 'For Shame'. Keep an eye on her mood, if she is distracted or annoyed try it some other time. Praise and treat her each time she removes the sticky note.

Think of a few situations where this command works in combination with a suitable sentence. E.g.

Lucy, I saw you running after a cat. Shame

Lucy, you didn't greet my friends. Shame.

Lucy, you created a mess for my mom. Shame.

Say it in normal voice and her cute act will make you forget her mistake.

Troubleshooting

This might take longer than usual for your puppy to pick up this command as the tape or sticky note serves as a distraction, but she'll get it.

Don't leave behind the tape or sticky note for your puppy to eat!

Greet (Hello or Goodbye)

Teach your puppy to say hello and wave goodbye to your friends and acquaintances. This command will make her super adorable.

You Need

Low-value treats, 'Paw' command.

Steps

Keep an empty hand open and visible for your puppy. Ask her to 'Paw' and when she raises her paw, raise your hand higher. She will try to reach your hand.

When she raises the paw higher, praise her and treat her.

Try this a few times and then gradually increase the height of your hand (raise her paw), until she raises up to her muzzle. When she raises her paw this high, add the command word 'Greet', praise and treat her. Repeat several times and reward her for each successful 'Greet'.

Subsequently, reduce and eliminate the treat and don't guide her with your hand. She will be greeting your friends from now on.

Troubleshooting
Greeting is not a natural movement for puppies, so be patient if the progress is slow. Practice a few times a day.

Clean Up
This command will train your puppy to tidy up the place after playtime.

You Need
A low height box, tray or basket for collecting toys, a few toys, high-value treats. 'Bring It', 'Drop It', 'Place' and 'Touch' commands already learnt.

Steps
Sit on the floor with the box near you. Draw your puppy's attention by calling her name.

Casually toss a toy a few feet away from you.

Point to the toy and ask her to 'Bring It'. When she is walking towards you with the toy in her mouth, point to the box without saying the command word.

As she reaches the box, holding the toy, ask her to 'Drop It'. Make sure her mouth was already at the opening of the box, so the toy drops in the box. For each successful collection, reward her with praise and a treat.

Repeat this exercise with different toys. Gradually increase the distance between you and the box and the distance you toss the toy, one thing at a time. Reward her more when she accomplishes this task.

When she has mastered the act, add the verbal command 'Clean Up'. Scatter a few toys and point to the box and ask her to 'Clean Up'. Make it a fun activity for her by not placing a lot of toys on the floor.

Troubleshooting
If your puppy gets confused initially and walks towards you instead of the box, place your hand on the box opening with your palm up. When she touches your hand, ask her to 'Drop It'. She will learn soon enough that she is being rewarded for dropping the toy in the box.

Frogger
Teach your puppy to jump over the objects.

You Need
High-value treats, a large enclosed area with enough run-up space, your helpers, 'Leap' and 'Stay' commands learnt.

Steps
One person creates a hurdle for the puppy by first kneeling and then squeezing their body in this shape. Their back should be flat parallel to the ground. Check that the person does not make a large obstacle for your puppy.

Stand on the other side of the person facing your puppy. Grab a high-value treat on your fist and let your puppy sniff it.

Ask your puppy to 'Stay' in her place, take a few steps back while you're still facing your helper and the puppy. Say 'Leap' and pull the treat backwards to you. If your puppy jumps over, practice this a few times. If she doesn't, practice the 'Leap' trick some more.

Now raise the 'bar' for your puppy, the point is to raise just a little bit every time your puppy practices and jumps. The aim is to reach a stance when your helper has the knees and hands on the ground and belly off the ground.

Once she is comfortable with jumping over the first helper, add another person at an appropriate distance. It's like a hurdle race where you have to jump over obstacles one after another. Give her lots of praises and treat when she jumps over both hurdles.

Now you can add more people or obstacles as long as they are all in a row and you give ample space for your puppy to run-up.

Troubleshooting
You use 'Leap-frogger' or 'Frogger' command word instead of 'Leap' if you want to teach your puppy to differentiate between single obstacle or multiple obstacle jump.

Puppies might jump over the back of your helper rather than fully jumping over them. Inform your helper that this could happen. Let them wear thick clothes so they don't get scratched by the paws.

This is an advanced trick and should not be played with young puppies. Secondly, keep an eye on her energy level and body language. Stop if she finds the hurdle too high or she feels tired.

Paws Up
Teach your puppy this cute stance where she holds her paws up sitting on hind legs.

You Need
High-value treats, 'Sit' command

Steps
Start by asking your puppy to 'Sit'. Grab a treat in each hand and hide your fists behind you.

Kneel and place both fist in front of you and let her smell them in sitting position.

Slowly raise your fists up. As soon as your puppy raises the front pays off the ground praise and give her a treat.

Practice until she can raise both of her paws up to her shoulder. Praise and give two treats for this achievement. Gradually increase the time second by second so she stays in this position for 10 seconds.

After she is consistent in this action, add the command word 'Paws Up'.

Troubleshooting
Timing is critical. You should mark the positive behavior as soon as she raises the paws, not when she has put them back on the floor.

Raise your hands in smooth motion so the puppy won't jump at the treat hand and lose her 'Sit' position. If she does that ignore her by turning away, wait a while and ask her to sit again. You should be patient with her as this is not a natural stance for a puppy.

Get Busy
This command will instruct your puppy to go for potty. Once learnt, this command can save accidents and keep your environment clean.

You Need
Walking gear (leash, harness, collar), high-value treats.

Steps

In the basic potty training, you leant to use a specific spot for potty and prepare your puppy to walk to that place.

Within that area, let her sniff and find a suitable place, don't let her drag to another place.

When she starts to pee or poop, say the command 'Get Busy'. This will connect the act with the word. You will praise and reward her for using the bathroom in the designated area.

Once you notice she has started connecting the command, you can try this at other appropriate places. This will teach her not to go in any public place but to use a designated or deserted place.

Troubleshooting
If she tries to relieve herself before you reach the spot, gently ask her to 'Sit' wait for a few seconds and continue to the spot and give 'Get Busy' command.

Since younger puppies don't have very good bladder control, choose a potty spot closer to your residence. You can move the spot farther away as your puppy grows.

If you follow a potty break routine, then you can not only avoid accidents but you can also know about the health status of your puppy. It is not a good idea to make your puppy hold onto her call of nature for a long time as it can make them sick.

Roll Over
You Need
Towel or blanket, low-value treats, 'Sit', 'Stay' and 'Down' commands.

Steps
Dogs generally feel unsafe when they are on their back but you can teach your puppy to 'Roll Over' with patience. Lay her favorite towel or blanket in front of you.

Ask her to 'Sit', 'Stay' and lie 'Down' on the blanket. Kneel in front of her. Hold the treat by the side of her muzzle. Slowly create a curve downward motion to lure your puppy to lie on her side.

Repeat the previous step several times from the 'Down' position. Treat her each time she lies on her side with the head on the floor. When she lies on her side, 10 times consecutively, move to the next level.

While your puppy is lying on her side take the treat from the side of her head, move it to the other side, keeping even motion. It's like creating a semicircle motion 180 degrees. When you move your hand upwards, try to make it closer to her chest so her mouth will follow your hand and her body will roll to the other side. You should give her double treat and lots of praises and affection when she is able to do it.

You can add the verbal command 'Roll Over' once she can roll over consistently.

Once she learns the verbal command you can try the hand movement without treat and while standing. You can even try different surfaces.

Troubleshooting
Your puppy must be familiar with the idea that you teach her different tricks and maneuvers. She should have a strong trust relationship with you for the advanced acts like 'Roll Over'.

Move your hand evenly and make sure your puppy knows what's hidden inside your fist. Move slowly so she can follow the smell. Use different treats to maintain her focus.

Fun and Games

Tug

Dogs love games and competition that keep them active. Tug-of-war is one such game. You must use appropriate type of rope though. The rope should be sufficiently thick, with several knots or a rubber tug toy appropriately sized for your puppy.

You Need

A rope or rubber tug toy

Steps

Show her one of the ropes ends to draw her attention. Show your excitement through your body language. Ask her to play. She might not understand a word you say but she will pick your excitement and fun time signal and grab one end of the rope. As she moves away from you, hold onto the other end tightly.

Now hold your ground as the competition has started already. She will pull and you pull against her. Keep the competition balanced

so she keeps interested and motivated. Lose deliberately by subtly letting go of the rope if she is not stronger.

Troubleshooting

Don't play tug with stuffed toys unless you want to clean-up the mess afterwards. The power struggle between you and your puppy will easily rip such toy apart.

If your puppy is possessive and would rather like an object thrown, then alternate between throwing a rope and tug toy to play.

The puppy might growl during tug and seem excited. This is normal unless she shows other signs of stress, fear or anxiety. If she is growling and other body language signs are positive, it's okay. If you are unsure if she is enjoying, ask an adult to help you decide.

Don't let go of the rope when she is actively pulling as this can cause her to roll backwards and hit a wall. To avoid hurting, let go of your end of rope only when you realize that she is not pulling with full strength and would be able to maintain balance.

If your puppy shows signs of aggression and possibly possessiveness, stop playing, let her have the toy, walk away and give her some time to cool down. Finally use 'Drop It' so she lets go of it and put it away from her.

Treasure Hunt

You will hide the treats in the absense of your puppy and she will use her nose to find and claim them.

You Need

Either high or low value treats (depending on the interest of the puppy), hiding places.

Steps

Confine your puppy in a room. You don't want her to know your hiding places.

Hide the treats in a few easy to find places.

Once done, open the door and let her find the hidden treats.

When she finds the first 'treasure' be excited and call her name and say 'found one' or any word that would tell her what game she's playing. She might not understand the words but she will see you being excited about it, so she would like it too.

Initially you might have to give her a 'guided tour' to point to the 'treasure' bits but when she develops an interest, she'll find them by herself. You can now replace the high value treats with low value ones.

Troubleshooting

If she comes out of the room and is confused as what to do, then guide her to the closest treat and then guide to the subsequent ones until she gets hold of this game.

For the safety of your puppy don't put the treats in unsafe or unhealthy places like in dirty corners, near the toilet. If you're playing outside make sure she doesn't discover unexpected 'treats' that you haven't placed for her.

Mix-up Cups

You Need

3 large plastic cups (large enough to hold a tennis ball or a toy), a toy, enough space for the fetch activity, 'Fetch', 'Drop It', 'Sit' and 'Down'.

Steps

Make her 'Sit' or lie 'Down'. Place the cups upside down in front of her at appropriate distance.

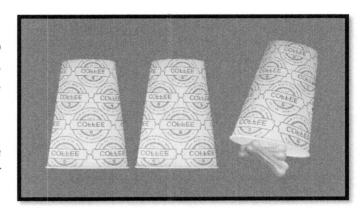

Place a toy she likes and hide it under any cup.

Now switch places and make it slow initially, once your puppy is interested in the game you can do it faster.

Once you stop, ask in an exciting voice, 'Where is it?'. She might knock the cup off with her paw or nose. Let her try until she finds the one.

When she finds it, show her the toy and throw it away. This 'Fetch' activity would be her reward for finding the right cup. When she brings it back ask her to 'Drop It' and continue playing.

Put the cups away when you are done as she might like to chew on them later.

Troubleshooting

For elder dogs you can use a tennis ball. If your puppy doesn't get it or is not interested then you can replace the tennis ball or toy with high value treat.

Runway House

You Need

An outdoor garden hose attached to a faucet, a hot day

Steps

Use an enclosed outdoor space. Bring your unleashed puppy with you.

Grab the hose and let her sniff before turning it on.

Slowly turn on the water. Make sure your puppy sees the water flowing.

Now aim the hose upward, away from the puppy and ask her to chase the water stream.

She will try to 'catch' the water stream, keep moving the hose direction.

Once you're done, let her shake off the water, dry with towel and the sunlight.

Troubleshooting

Do this in a sunny day when the temperature is high as the puppies will be super scared if they are feeling cold and you put cold water on them.

Introduce the hose slowly until your puppy gets used to it. If you directly expose her to a full on hose, she could be scared of it for good.

Don't spray directly at her face, as she would be scared.

Don't use a leash in this activity as the puppy should be free to move.

If your puppy shows signs of distress, like cowering, tucking their tails between the legs or laying ears against her head, stop playing. Choose another game to play.

Muffin Pan Game

You Need

High-value treats, muffin pan, small toys or tennis balls (as many toys as there are slots in the pan)

Steps

We have to setup the pan before the puppy sees the pan. Fill about one third slots with treats. Cover all the holes with toys or tennis balls.

Place the tray on the floor and call her up.

Let her find out which of the toys is hiding treats. It's fun to watch her play. Keep playing until both of you are interested.

Wash the pan with a detergent before returning it.

Troubleshooting

If your puppy doesn't get it, tap the toy and say in upbeat voice, 'Hey, what's this!'. If she still is shy of removing the toy and exploring under it, remove one of toy with treats under it and put it back.

Once she is familiar with the game you can replace the high-value treats with low-value ones.

Some puppies prefer to play with the toys or tennis ball, ignoring the treats underneath. It's fine as long as she is happy, we're happy.

Make sure you get permission to use the pan and wash the pan thoroughly right away. You don't want to take a chance of exchanging germs from animal world to yours.

Bubble Catch

You make bubbles and your puppy tries to catch. Most puppies love to pop the bubbles and follow them.

one illustration only. a puppy holding a bubble in her mouth and one or two more bubbles around her.

You Need

Bubble solution and bubble wand

Steps

Make a bubble or two to start with. You don't want to confuse your puppy with lots of them. Encourage her to notice the bubble and chase it.

Catch a bubble and let her sniff and pop it. Once she gets hold of it, let the bubbles float!

Troubleshooting

Don't blow bubbles in her face.

Don't play for too long as your puppy is consuming detergent in tiny droplets that can total up to a significant amount. Although the game was fun but her mouth will taste bad after this. Offer her lots of water to drink to wash out the taste.

This is an outdoor game but if you play inside, ask permission and cleanup the floor with towel as the floor could be slippery afterwards.

Fetch

Dogs are natural hunters, retrievers, chasers and runners. This can be played indoor or outdoor. While playing indoor, make sure you have ample space for your puppy to run without bumping into a delicate object.

a puppy fetching a tennis ball or toy ball in her mouth running across.

You Need

A favorite ball or toy, 'Drop It' and 'Sit' commands

Steps

Decide the place where you want to play. Choose a toy of your puppy's liking.

Draw her attention by calling her or showing the toy.

Ask her to 'Sit' and then toss the object away. She will rush to get it.

Once she gets hold of it, call her back and use 'Drop It' to drop so that you can throw it again.

Troubleshooting

Initially your puppy might get the toy and start playing with it rather than coming back to you. If she doesn't return, be patient and keep calling her at appropriate intervals.

Don't snatch the object from her mouth if she doesn't let go.

Depending on the space available, you would want to toss rather than throw, when playing indoor.

Frisbee

This is an exclusively outdoor activity. We will let the puppy fetch the frisbee and soon she would be able to catch it as well.

You Need

A frisbee, an outdoor space.

Steps

Ask the puppy to 'Sit' and hold the frisbee out for them to see and smell but don't give it to them.

Toss it at a short distance.

Initially she might not catch it, rather just pick it up and bring it back. Ask her to 'Drop It' and appreciate her.

Gradually increase the distance.

Troubleshooting
Some dog breeds learn frisbee quickly and try to catch it by jumping at it. Some rather like to bring it back.

Don't throw the frisbee beyond an obstacle like a car, bushes or fence etc. as your puppy would be following frisbee in the air and might not notice the obstacle ahead of her.

Soccer

You Need
A soccer ball, high-value treats

Steps
Start in a quiet empty indoor space. Let the puppy smell it and she might paw the ball in an attempt to explore it. Praise her and give her a treat.

Every time she moves the ball, praise her and treat her. Repeat this activity a few times to establish that playing with the soccer ball is appreciated.

Now kneel on the floor, roll the ball under your hand back and forth. When your puppy is paying attention to it, roll it towards her. If she changes the direction of the ball, praise and offer her treat. Repeat this a few times.

Up the level by taking it outside and repeating the previous exercise again. This time you can roll the ball gently under your foot while standing and gently pushing towards her. Never kick hard directly towards her. You don't want to hurt your soccer pal.

Once she gets hold of it, you can play co-op where she would pass the ball back and forth. You could also try to dodge her and she would do the same!

Troubleshooting
Like frisbee, some breeds are natural at soccer but you can teach any breed nonetheless.

Choose the size of soccer ball according to the size of your puppy.

Roll It

You Need
Low-value treats, a marker, scissors or a cutter, an empty plastic bottle with a cap, an adult to supervise

Steps
First, we will create the resource for this game, a rolling object that dispenses treats. Take the bottle and carve about 3 holes in different directions. The holes should be slightly larger than the kibble or treat used. If the holes are too large, they will dispense all the treats in one place without rolling much. If the holes are too small it would not dispense the treats at all. An adult can help you or supervise you in this step. Make sure the cut-out holes don't have sharp edges. Place a few low-value treats in it.

Now it's time to test it. Securely close the lid or cap. Roll the bottle on the floor gently. It should roll dispensing a few treats on the floor.

Draw the attention of your puppy by shaking the bottle and placing it flat on the floor. Watch her as she figures out how to dispense the treats by rolling it.

Troubleshooting
Adjust the size of the holes, if the treats dispense too quickly (means holes are too large) or the treats won't come out (means the holes are too small). You can make the holes smaller by adding paper padding around the holes. You can carve them more to make them larger.

This activity will help the puppies who devour their food viciously. After this activity they might slow down at mealtime.

Remove the 'rolling dispenser' from the play area. Your puppy should not have access to it outside of controlled playtime.

Hide & Seek

You Need
'Sit' and 'Stay' commands already learnt, another person to help in the beginning.

Steps
Hide and seek is a fun game that can be played indoor or outdoor. Remember that you get to hide almost everytime and your puppy will find you. Decide a place to play.

Assign a place for your puppy to 'Sit' and 'Stay'. This place should be used consistently so she would know this is my goto place for hide and seek.

Now go and hide somewhere. If she tries to follow you, ask someone to make her 'Sit' and 'Stay'.

In your hiding place, call up your puppy. You might have have to call her over and over with appropriate intervals before she gets to you. It would become more obvious for her as she learns to play.

When she finds you, show excitement, praise and appreciate her. Repeat the steps until she learns that she should not move from her location until you call her name.

Troubleshooting

Sometime your puppy might be exhausted, bored or simply distracted. You can continue calling her to remind her she's still 'in' the game.

Choose the hiding spot wisely as your puppy might assume these spots to be safe. Don't hide in tiny spaces with less oxygen, inside a container or electrical equipment like washing machine, refrigerator, inside cupboard. Choose simple places to hide so she could find you.

Flip It

You Need

Empty soft drink bottles without cap, low value treats, marker, scissors or knife, 3 feet long stick, 2 kitchen chairs (optional), adult supervision

Steps

We will create a custom toy for our puppy, just like 'Roll It'. She will flip the to receive treats. This time we will not make holes for the treats, instead we will create two holes across at the top of the bottle neck so that the stick can run through it.

Cut the marked areas in all bottles. Check the cut-out holes if their edges are smooth.

Place all the bottles through the stick. Test if you can flip the bottles freely.

Put some treats in each of the bottles and show this setup to your puppy. Let her figure out how she can receive the treat by flipping the bottle. If she seems frustrated about the treats that she can see but not get it, then help her by showing how flipping the bottle will dispense the treat. Once she gets it, she'll love it.

Troubleshooting

The stick should be secure and the pedestal used should be strong. If the chairs used are lightweight (made with plastic or fiber), the whole setup could collapse.

Determine the number of bottles, length of stick and height of stick, according to the size of your puppy.

Clean up after this activity and hide this toy from her as once treats are consumed, she might start chewing at the bottles.

Find It

It's a fun game to enjoy time with your puppy. You can play it indoor or outdor. You can think of it as a more discreet version of 'Bring It'.

You Need

Low-value treats, your puppy's favorite toy.

Steps

Show the puppy her favorite toy to increase her interest.

Hide it away somewhere in the house. Make sure she doesn't see you hiding the toy. You could also confine her in a room if she follows you around.

Let her out and ask her to 'Bring It'.

Join her and pretend to be looking for it and keep her engaged and focused.

If it takes too long for her to find, you can guide her closer to the toy. Try not to point directly towards the toy as it won't be fun, let her discover it.

When she finds it, praise and give treat to her.

Troubleshooting

Your puppy might be confused initially as to what you want from her. Your body language and consistent encouragement will let her know what you want.

You can have 5-6 pre-determined hiding spots. It will make the game easier and more fun for the puppy.

Don't hide the toy in hard to access places like inside the closet (even if the door is open). Similarly, don't place the object near fragile objects (like flower pots) or on shelves or pedestals.

The Name Game

You might have noticed that your puppy has already learnt a few commands and has started to recognize people and objcts by their names.

A kid standing beside a schoolbag pointing to it and saying 'schoolbag' in speech bubble. A puppy saying 'schoolbag' in thought bubble moving towards the bag. (not to scale)

You Need

Pen and paper, high-value treats, the names you want her to know (people, objects, places)

Steps

List a few names you want your puppy to recognize. We'll go slow and teach her one item at a time.

For today, pick a name from the list. Let's say you want to teach them 'schoolbag'.

Decide a starting point for this activity. Make a mental note of this place as you will keep coming back to this place. While standing in front of your puppy, draw her attention by calling her name. Place the bag next to you and say 'schoolbag' while pointing towards the bag.

Now move the bag a couple of feet away. Address your puppy by calling her by her name, then ask, 'Where's the schoolbag?'. Once you have her attention, walk over to the bag and say again pointing to the bag 'Schoolbag'.

Return back to your 'base'. Repeat this exercise while moving the bag to different places.

After practice, when you ask 'Where's the schoolbag?' and your puppy looks at it or walks next to it, give them praises and treat. If she is confused and doesn't do either of the actions, move close to the bag and re-introduce it by saying 'schoolbag'.

Repeat the last step over and over until she links the word 'schoolbag' with the physical object. For next few weeks, casually ask her 'Where's the schoolbag?' at random times to confirm she has learnt it. On every successful response give her praise and a treat.

If you go slow, you can teach her a lot of words and introduce many people. The 'objects' part is best as you can ask her to bring your 'schoolbag', 'newspaper' etc.

Troubleshooting

Pace your vocabulary drills according to your puppy's capability. Additionally, keep using these words or names repeatedly else she might forget. When you play reminder games, give her praise or treats.

Be mindful of the people and objects you introduce your puppy to. If you want her to keep away from an object or not to pay attention to it, don't include it in her vocabulary. Avoid people and things that are harmful or hazardous for her or are too fragile or susceptible to break.

Hurdle Dash

This is an amazing activity for your puppy if they know the basic manuvers like 'Leap' and 'Tunnel'.

You Need

An adult supervisor, pen and paper, a long stick, 2 wooden blocks or a stack of books, hula hoop, 2 outdoor chairs, large cardboard box, plywood, a large flat rock, 6 different colored painted sticks about 2 feet long, 'Leap' and 'Tunnel' commands.

Steps

You will design hurdles course on a piece of paper. Measure the outdoor space available to you. Spread out the objects sparcely in the space available as you want your puppy to have enough space and time to evade next hurdle.

A hula hoop could be a good starting point. You could hold it or place it between two chairs.

Cut open a cardboard box from top and bottom. If weather conditions are windy in your area place rocks or stones or books on both sides so it won't move with the wind. Make sure the rocks are not too large that your puppy bumps into them.

Setup stick on top of your wooden blocks or stack of books (same setup as 'Leap').

Setup a ramp by placing a plywood on rock. Make sure that it doesn't shake when your pup gets on it. Adjust accordingly by placing more stones.

Considering the size of your puppy, place painted sticks on the ground in a straight line.

Encourage your puppy to overcome one hurdle at a time. Once she practices enough, move to another hurdle. Show her the zig-zag movement by first doing it yourself through the painted sticks. Praise her and treat her on each step.

If she finds any hurdle hard to manage skip it for now and visit late or skip this altogether. This should be fun for her too. You can share a video of her doing these neat tricks!

Troubleshooting

Go slow and introduce one trick at a time. Skip the ones that are too hard for her or she doesn't like.

You can re-arrange the hurdles as you wish.

Discuss and seek help of an adult in the setup. Make it safe for the puppy. Don't make jumping task too high that she might trip over her hindlegs. There should be no sharp or pointy edges.

Notes for parents

1. Having a pet is a very positive activity that one can have. Encourage your child and help them along. Don't lose patience with both your child and the pet. Children might need help frequently.

2. If you think that your dog or puppy is behaving abnormally, especially towards your child, consult a veterinarian or behavior specialist immediately to avoid any potential harm.

3. Usually we think that children are bitten by unfamiliar and stranger dogs, although that is less common than kids being bit by their own pets if they are uncomfortable around each other and can't communicate well. So be careful and maintain proper supervision.

4. Kids can do some grooming jobs on their own like brushing, but some jobs require some level of restrain and can be uncomfortable for the dog. So, they are better done by parents or other adults. Examples of these jobs are: ear cleaning, nail trimming and tooth brushing.

5. You would need to carefully observe the dog's mouthing and distinguish between normal licking and mouthing and more deliberate nipping which is dangerous. It can become hurtful biting when the puppy grows older and has sharp teeth. You should contact your vet or trainer immediately if you see signs of aggressive biting.

6. If your dog is growling, especially at a child, don't stop or punish it instantly. Instead, remember that usually a dog only growls when it's pushed over the corner, so try to fix the problem from the root. Ask the child about what they did to the dog. And try to figure out the real problem. Sometimes a child maybe annoying the puppy unintentionally.

7. Help your children in training their puppy but let them do most of the work. Don't tell them away if they ask you for help in something. They may try to do it by themselves. Just support them and don't overrule.

8. Provide them with proper equipment and avoid low quality food and other supplies. Consider your budget for your puppy beforehand to avoid problems later.

9. Consider some things before letting your child walk the dog on their own. Some of these are:
   a. Can your child handle the dog with ease? Would they handle it if the dog starts to pull in the leash?
   b. Is the environment and neighborhood safe? Is there a dedicated walking path available?
   c. How much traffic is usually on the road?
   d. Is the traffic slow? Are there any heavy vehicles allowed?
   e. How often do you find stray cats? It's common knowledge that dogs tend to try and chase them which can be a problem for your child.
   f. Are your child and their dog close enough? Can they communicate properly, and are they comfortable with each other?

1. Puppies can get aggressive about their food or some other things. The reasons for this can be a little complicated so if you see any troubling signs, contact a trainer or vet as soon as possible as this behavior can get worse.

Puppy Walk Schedule

Day		Morning	Mid-Morning	Midday	Evening	Night-time
Monday	**Time**					
	Pee	☐	☐	☐	☐	☐
	Poop	☐	☐	☐	☐	☐
Tuesday	**Time**					
	Pee	☐	☐	☐	☐	☐
	Poop	☐	☐	☐	☐	☐
Wednesday	**Time**					
	Pee	☐	☐	☐	☐	☐
	Poop	☐	☐	☐	☐	☐
Thursday	**Time**					
	Pee	☐	☐	☐	☐	☐
	Poop	☐	☐	☐	☐	☐
Friday	**Time**					
	Pee	☐	☐	☐	☐	☐
	Poop	☐	☐	☐	☐	☐
Saturday	**Time**					
	Pee	☐	☐	☐	☐	☐
	Poop	☐	☐	☐	☐	☐
Sunday	**Time**					
	Pee	☐	☐	☐	☐	☐
	Poop	☐	☐	☐	☐	☐

* this is a standard template. You can use it as is and you can also use the following template chart where you can mark the time by yourself.

** remember not to give very long breaks between walks. For puppies between 12 to 24 months, 3-hour break might be sufficient and for older dogs you can take it up to 6 to 8 hours. Make sure you know your puppy's habit first and different breeds have different bladder size and control.

Day		Morning	Mid-Morning	Midday	Evening	Night-time
		6:00 AM	9:00 AM	12:00 PM	6:00 PM	9:00 PM
Monday	Time					
	Pee	☐	☐	☐	☐	☐
	Poop	☐	☐	☐	☐	☐
Tuesday	Time					
	Pee	☐	☐	☐	☐	☐
	Poop	☐	☐	☐	☐	☐
Wednesday	Time					
	Pee	☐	☐	☐	☐	☐
	Poop	☐	☐	☐	☐	☐
Thursday	Time					
	Pee	☐	☐	☐	☐	☐
	Poop	☐	☐	☐	☐	☐
Friday	Time					
	Pee	☐	☐	☐	☐	☐
	Poop	☐	☐	☐	☐	☐
Saturday	Time					
	Pee	☐	☐	☐	☐	☐
	Poop	☐	☐	☐	☐	☐
Sunday	Time					
	Pee	☐	☐	☐	☐	☐
	Poop	☐	☐	☐	☐	☐

Disclaimer

Dogs are living and breathing creatures that can be unpredictable in their nature. For this reason, there is always a relative risk and volatility in working with any animal, known or unknown.

Although the authors and publishers have made every effort to ensure that the information in this book was correct at press time, the authors and publishers do not assume and hereby disclaim any liability to any party for any loss, damage, or disruption caused by application of information, errors or omissions, whether such errors or omissions result from negligence, accident, or any other cause.

This book is not intended as a substitute for the medical or training professionals. The reader should regularly consult a physician in matters relating to health and particularly with respect to any symptoms that may require diagnosis or medical attention.

The information in this book is meant to supplement, not replace, proper dog training. Like any other hobby or sport or activity, dog training poses some inherent risk. The authors and publisher advise readers to take full responsibility for their safety and know their limits. Before practicing the skills described in this book, make sure that your equipment is in order, and do not take risks beyond your level of experience, aptitude, training, and comfort level.

The information contained within this book is presented for educational purposes only. Authors and publishers make no warranties of any kind, express or implied, about the completeness, accuracy, reliability, suitability, or availability of the book or the information, images, services, products, and other content of the book. By using this book, you consent to use the information contained therein at your own risk. At no time will authors/publishers be liable for any loss or damage that results, directly or indirectly, from your use of the information, services, products, or contents of this book.

Printed in Great Britain
by Amazon

79422746R00052